BARBARA SHER'S IDEA BOOK

How to Discover What You Really Want
(Even if You Have No Clue)

Barbara Sher

Book One in her new series
How To Do What You Love Without Starving to Death

Genius Press Unltd.
www.geniuspress.com
New York

Barbara Sher's Idea Book ....
1st edition
ISBN 0-9728952-0-5
copyright © 2004 by Barbara Sher

DEDICATION

To all human beings who long to do what they love
and still pay the rent.

Also by Barbara Sher

BOOKS

Wishcraft

Teamworks!

I Could Do Anything if I Only Knew What It Was

Live the Life You Love

It's Only Too Late if You Don't Start Now

AUDIO COURSES

Dare to Live Your Dream 12-audiocassette course

Discover Your Dream Workbook with audio CD

VIDEOS FOR PUBLIC TELEVISION

How To Create Your Second Life After 40

Live the Life You Love/Map To Success

Barbara Sher's Idea Party

ACKNOWLEDGEMENTS

To Matthew Pearl, a first-rate editor, writer, researcher and proofreader, who worked with me almost every day for two years to turn my scraps, notes and emails into books and who is an unending pleasure to work with, I say, "Bless you and yours. Take the rest of the week off and then let's do another one!"

To Andrea Reese, my trusted assistant, who always lifted my spirits, changed her life to meet my writing schedule and took the office load off my shoulders to give me what every writer can only dream of: free time to write, I give my sincerest thanks.

Together these two people created the perfect team and gave me the happiest writing experience I've had so far. Best of all, both of them are living their dreams in addition to helping me live mine—Matt in Greece with his wife and their fine baby, Leo; Andrea with the continuing success of her one-woman play, Cirque Jacqueline.

Thanks to all my wonderful Success Team leaders around the world who work every day to help people achieve their goals and who sent me some terrific success stories to share with you. Many thanks to all the wizards on my bulletin board who continually give intelligent, heartfelt help to everyone who asks for it and who are so knowledgeable I am always astounded. They generously gave me permission to share some of their best information with you.

Finally, a huge thanks to all the people who requested ideas via letters, private sessions, telephone Idea Parties, Success Teams and my workshops (to say nothing of taxis, restaurants and airplanes). You have allowed me (and everyone who stepped forward to help) to do what we love most: scout for creative solutions, cheer you on with our personal experiences, share our information and address books, and dig around for some way, by hook or by crook, to make your dreams come true. I hope this book, in sharing the results of all that jolly brainstorming, will spread your success to many more dreamers.

"I don't want to sell anything, buy anything or process anything,
as a career.

I don't want to sell anything bought or processed,
or process anything sold, bought
or processed,

or buy anything sold or processed.

Or process anything sold,
bought
or processed.

Or repair anything
sold, bought or processed.

You know, as a career.
I don't want to do that."

John Cusak's character in the 1989 movie "Say Anything"

CONTENTS

INTRODUCTION

"What book are you working on now, Barbara?" one of the security officers at LaGuardia Airport called out on one of my recent trips. He sees me so often we've become old friends. This time he was standing at a different screening machine about six feet away and the airport was noisy.

"This one's about how to do what you love without starving to death!" I called out.

Every person in both lines stopped and looked at me.

Now, you understand that when you shout in New York, people don't stop and look at you. It must have been what I said.

The security officer who was screening my luggage leaned forward. "Can we talk? I really have to come up with something. I don't want to leave my kids alone all the time," she whispered.

The man in front of me with a computer half way out of his briefcase stepped out of line and handed me his card, saying, "Email me?"

"Where can we get the book?" the woman behind me asked. "When will it be in bookstores?"

Obviously, I had struck a chord.

I have always loved books packed with ideas for interesting and unusual ways to earn money. Even before I began running Idea Parties and Success Team workshops in 1975, I had a sizeable collection of books devoted to the subject: *365 Ways To Earn A Living Without a Job, Dollars at Your Doorstep, 100 Businesses You Can Start with $1000.* I still look through them periodically, although many of their suggestions are outdated. (Many are now out of print, but thanks to the internet you can usually get your hands on them anyway. Just do a search for "used books".)

But most of the ideas in this book come from the work I do every day. The major part, my favorite part of what I do—in private sessions, telephone classes, television shows, in workshops or wherever someone recognizes me and strikes up a conversation—is to try to find ideas that allow impossible-looking dreams to come true. The routine usually goes like this:

I ask, "So what do you want to be when you grow up?" and they reply, "I don't know."

So far, that's never been true. Within minutes we've established that either: 1) they know perfectly well what they want but it seems so impossible they've never seriously considered it; or 2) they want too many things and can't choose just one.

I can usually dispose of the second scenario in a few seconds: "Who said you were supposed to choose one? Do them all." The results are delightful and immediate. The first response is silence and an expression like a corralled horse that just noticed the gate was open. Then they grin and you can almost hear them thinking, "Oh, right!" and they look as though a huge weight has fallen off their shoulders.

The first scenario goes a lot deeper, however. So, why do their dreams seem so impossible? Because, like most of us, they make assumptions based on conventional wisdom that stop their dreams before they leave the starting gate. They assume everything they want to do has to earn money, usually in the form of a paycheck. Or they think it costs a lot of money: their dream of having a bed and breakfast means they have to buy a Victorian house. People automatically assume they need fancy credentials, when not only don't they need them, but having credentials could put them on a track where jobs are actually harder to find. And they make lots of other assumptions, too. They're too old, there's no market for what they want to sell, they have no time...that kind of thing.

That covers about 99% of what people ask me to help them with. I've found the very best way to help is to run lots of brand new ideas past them, the kinds of ideas that bust their assumptions wide open and show how narrow and inaccurate conventional wisdom really is.

So many dreams die unnecessarily. People give up because they just don't have enough information: People from corporations assume that there's only one way to go into business and it's loaded with business plans, bank loans and investors. People from academia always assume you need advanced credentials for anything you want to do. And yet, there are people doing exactly what they love, making decent money doing it, without business plans, bank loans, a 9-5 job or an advanced degree.

So if you're someone who thinks it's impossible to do what you really want (without starving to death), it's time for some fresh thinking. You need a different approach, new angles, innovative strategies. That is to say, you need lots and lots of ideas to give you truly original ways to do all kinds of things.

Fresh ideas are delightful entities and they're absolutely necessary to start planning a path to a goal you will be happy with. Of course, even a really good idea won't bring the hay in, as my country neighbors often tell me. Not to worry. Once you've found some ideas that wake up your interest, this book will give you a first-rate method for adapting them to your personal specifications. (Take a peek at Appendix 2: Idea Soup. It's a honey.)

But you have to start by letting your imagination have some fun, to play a little, and even do a few minutes of fantasizing or pretending. This isn't just a good idea. It's essential. Every time you come across an idea in this book that makes you perk up and get interested—or one that just looks like fun—you've stumbled on a marker, a clue from your genetic finger-print, your biological makeup. Your receptiveness to the ideas in this book is your own kind of private genome mapping. You were designed with some special abilities you might not be aware of, but they are what draw you to one idea instead of another. Remember, what you love is what you are gifted at. Anything that looks like a good idea to you must be noted. I've left wide outside margins so you can note your H-Level at any point where it seems relevant. That is, if something looks just great, write "HL 9" or "9" in the margin next to it. If it looks unusually detestable, write "HL 2".

What's an "H-Level"? Briefly, "H" stands for Happiness. Assigning H-Levels to anything—a color, a food or a lifestyle—is a surprisingly precise (and easy!) way of figuring out which elements in any idea appeal to you. On a scale of 1 to 10, if 1 is dismal and 10 is pure heaven, you can assign with good-enough accuracy how you feel about any aspect of the ideas you'll be reading in these pages. The numbers you write on these pages can give you amazing insights into talents you may not have noticed, or even thought of as talents. H-Levels reveal elements that can become the building blocks to a happy and productive life for you. If anything is a 7 or greater, that means it's very important and must be noted. Be sure to circle it and write the actual H-Level next to it.

The next section, HOW TO USE THIS BOOK, will help you pull the most from my decisions on how to organize this material. But I'd like to explain my choice here in the Introduction. After many tries, I've decided to lay the ideas out alphabetically, which means, actually, that they have no logical structure at all.

There's no particular significance to the fact that "Coaching," for example, starts with a "C". Alphabetical ordering means that "Gondolier" probably won't come before or after anything related to it. That's because I want you to encounter these ideas in no logical order, without a hierarchy to show you what's most important, what's less important, and which activities should be grouped together. The reason? This is an idea book, and ideas are unruly, beautiful things. Like small, fast birds they dart in any direction at all.

Most importantly, the best way I can get you to stir up fresh ideas of your own is by presenting mine in the most random fashion. I'm hoping this alphabetical organization will help to stimulate that part of your brain that loves possibilities and scorns practicality. The lack of logic in the order in which you read the pages, even the absence of continuity, will hopefully wake up your own nice, messy, untamed ideas.

Give your brain a chance to do its best work by respecting and jotting down all the thoughts that pop into your mind in the spaces I've left for you, and take the time to answer the questions I've asked.

Also keep your eyes open for the "meta-dream" that fills the hearts of so many people—not any particular activity, but something else that is crucially important to their happiness: to live by the ocean or in the mountains, or simply to never work at a formal "job" again. If that's you, what's needed is some way to support that lifestyle financially. You'll find some excellent ideas for how to do that as you read through these pages—ideas that will turn that "impossible dream" into a day-to-day reality.

One more point: Not all of the following ideas are designed to make money (although they definitely could); they're about using your talents and gifts to their fullest—and starting as soon as possible. Some of your talents are of such importance that they shouldn't be compromised or made to justify themselves financially. You shouldn't re-make them so they'll earn money in the marketplace. Instead, these activities can be subsidized by earning money some other way, and I've come up with as many ways as I can think of to keep you in groceries and with a roof over your head, even if you're a poet, an artist, or a philosopher.

Other dreams can make money and should. You'll find lots of wonderfully ingenious approaches to earning money doing what you love in the following pages.

If you can and wish to turn your dream into a small business or some form of self-employment, I have chosen ideas that require almost no risk (that is, no investment, no loans, no expensive rents, and no full-time employees for you to worry about). These ideas don't require that you go to school for years to get advanced degrees, either. The best ideas are those which will be fun and use skills that come easily to you. Not just so you'll have a good time (though that's very important), but because when things are fun and the learning curve is an easy one, we tend to be more flexible and inventive. A small, enjoyable endeavor that doesn't succeed will leave you with energy and enthusiasm to try another, and it will always give you knowledge you didn't have before. Why get worn out at the School of Hard Knocks when you can attend the School of Enjoyable Exploration and increase your chances of persisting until you find what you're looking for?

Incidentally, turning a beloved activity into a small business doesn't mean you have to do everything from scratch (or buy, build and sell everything yourself and be your entire office staff, as well). Discovering what you're best at and finding ingenious, low-cost ways of delegating everything else is the first art of a successful business owner. The "Lone Ranger" assumption makes too many people abandon marvelous dreams.

And the assumption that "Everything Has to Be Big!" is foolish and wasteful. It kills almost as many brilliant ideas as the Lone Ranger assumption.

For example, during an off-camera break on a recent television show, one of the women who had been on camera with me sighed and said, "My son often tells me I should incorporate and start my own business. Maybe someday I'll get around to it. But it's such a huge project."

Guessing that she and her son had made the dream bigger than it needed to be, I asked, "What kind of a business would you start?"

"A garden center," she answered, smiling dreamily. "But who has the time or money to start up a project so big?"

"What's the part of that business you'd enjoy the most?" I asked.

Her smile broadened and her eyes lit up. "I love finding neglected or badly designed gardens and turning them into gorgeous ones!" she said.

Now, I know from many years of experience that when someone's eyes light up and they smile while talking about a dream, that's their gift speaking. (It's just like H-Levels, in fact, but visible to outsiders.)

"Why start such a big business?" I asked. "Why not start small, maybe even stay small? First, find a couple of friends with unfortunate gardens, get a photographer to shoot some good photos of how the garden looks now and follow what you do about it, then take a few weeks or months to make the garden gorgeous. That's your portfolio. You can use it to get an article written about you in a local newspaper, and you can also take it to your favorite garden center and tell the owner that if he'll promote your services, you'll use his products. You can even lecture at the garden center and bring in business for both of you. That way you won't need to incorporate anything, or own inventory, or pay rent on a building. You don't even have to quit the job you presently have. And you can start taking the first steps tomorrow."

She listened with surprise. Then she started to look very happy as she realized she didn't have to wait or take on a huge project (or a huge financial risk) to do what she loved at all. She could pick up the phone, call a friend, get a photographer and start on her dream in a few days.

That's how fresh ideas can make dreams come true, and there's nothing in the world more enjoyable. (I just felt a smile on *my* face while I was writing that story.)

If, for example, you want to work at home (or need to), and if, like a woman I know, what you really love is something as "impractical" as ancient Greek and Roman literature, you don't have to seek a job in a school. You can open a nice little home business tutoring kids on the internet. Just put up a website (you can get free or nearly-free ones.) A website will let you show off a bit where people can watch you. You can also have a bulletin board for free questions and answers. You can offer telephone tutoring while Ovid is up on your computer screen, or you can ask and answer questions on Instant Messaging if you'd like to tutor someone overseas and save money on your phone calls. You can send out a brief email newsletter to your students telling about some of the things you've been asked and have answered in the previous week.

If your tutoring service doesn't earn all the income you need, you can add some more services to your repertoire in completely different fields, depending on your skills and interests. If you're good with numbers, you can do tax preparation for artists in February and March and run a small lawn care service agency in the summer (hiring other people to do the actual work.)

Or, perhaps you're like Elise who had a good job but couldn't bear to be away from her pre-school children every day. She asked to work part time and the company actually said yes, but the household would be short of income if she stopped working full time. She was stuck. Or was she? A group of friends got together to brainstorm her dilemma, and discovered that she owned a nice big van. That changed everything. She went on a part-time schedule at her company and started a special neighborhood pickup and delivery service—and took her children with her everywhere she went.

If you're a writer who also needs to eat, you can be a freelance writing teacher in a corporation or for the military and make up to $4,000 a day. Yes, that's real. It's done all the time. Look at this article I read in "Writers Digest Magazine" a few years ago:

"With fees ranging from $100 to $4,000 a day, teaching writing often pays better than writing itself. Here are some steps you can take to join the lucrative speaking, consulting, training seminar and workshop business...A few weeks ago I taught a writing seminar to a group of 25 logistics professionals employed by the US Army. My fee: $6,000. The week before, I taught a shorter version of the seminar at a medical equipment company. For less than a day's work, I received $3,500 plus expenses.

"The point: writers can earn significant fees teaching their writing and marketing skills to others. In fact, surveys frequently cite writing and other communications skills as key factors contributing to the success of corporate managers and support staff. Yet many executives will tell you their employees are poor writers. This creates a steady demand for in-house corporate seminars that teach basic writing skills, business and technical writing, grammar, and presentation skills. Specialty subjects, such as how to write reports, manuals and proposals, are also in demand..."

Robert Bly "Teach and Grow Rich"

(You can find the whole article at *www.bly.com/Pages/writersonly/Teach*)

Now, that's what I call a good idea.

Ideas have power. They can change your life. In the following pages, you'll find ways to earn money without holding down a soul-sucking job, or ways to support your dreams even if they don't earn money, or ideas for going after dreams you thought cost money but don't—even some great ways to simply get your hands on some quick cash when you need it.

However, if you really have dreams of business plans, big investors, IPOs and a place on NASDAQ, you probably should find another book, and there are many of them available for you in the business section of any bookstore or library. Many of the ideas here will show you how to make money, of course. But not huge amounts. Getting rich isn't a goal in this book. Why not? Because almost everyone wants to get rich in order to do something they love with the money, and I have ideas that will get you what you love without the money. So why waste your time getting rich? Why not go directly to your dream and bypass the years of trying to gather wealth?

Different dreamers have different needs

What if your problem isn't about money, but indecision or an unwillingness to focus on only one thing? Well, if you like to write, you can write books or articles about anything that takes your fancy—whales this month, archaeology or filmmaking next month. What if you can't get your articles published? Then start your own e-zine on the internet where people can see your articles, and shoot emails past the noses of magazines to show them what they're missing while you find another temporary way to make your living. Or you can be an Information Specialist (see "I" for Information Broker) and do research for your clients in every field that exists. (You can shoot emails past appropriate noses in this case, too. Every time you find an amazing piece of information that's not relevant to the search you're doing at the time, send it to people who will notice. Be sure to sign it with your email address along with a catchy handle, like "The Obsessive Researcher".)

Or become a freelance teacher and teach anything that interests you. Unlike a teacher in an institution, you can change what you teach every semester and never get bored. What school will let you do a thing like that? Adult Education centers like the Learning Annex in New York and other cities in the U.S. and Canada. Do they pay enough for you to live? No, they don't, but they bring students into your classes who can later become private students or clients. I know of three separate cases where a teacher at adult education groups was asked by a group of attendees to teach a private, ongoing class which added hundreds of dollars to their weekly incomes.

And what if you're someone who's interested in lots of different things? You can self-publish e-books on any subject you love, on your own without any special software (see "P" for Publishing). If you think having too many interests makes you a "Jack of all trades, master of none," here's an author who tells you how to become an expert authority in any one field and has written dozens of special information books, each on a separate subject! Author Stephen J. Spignesi, has written *The Complete Stephen King Encyclopedia, The Complete Titanic* and a novel-in-progress called *Shelter Street,* among over a dozen other books! (and the next time someone tries to call you a dilettante, direct them to Leonardo da Vinci, Isaac Asimov or Ben Franklin).

Support that dream

But what if the one thing you love will *never* bring in money? I know someone who wants to be a poet, and writing poetry is no way to pay the rent. Poems don't sell and poets shouldn't write them to sell anyway: they should simply write the best they can. This poet needs a non-toxic job that uses up to eight hours of his day and no more, preferably less. With a day job, he can dedicate his free hours to writing poetry without worrying about paying the bills. (He'll join the ranks of the most notable American poets who had other jobs: Wallace Stevens spent his days at an insurance office and William Carlos Williams was a physician).

Eleanor wants to pursue her photography and she wants to get paid for it. She doesn't want a "good-enough job" during the day. She needs to find some good ideas for turning her passion into good income (See Mindy's story below in Part One: Idea Warm Up).

Alan left his law practice (even though he doesn't mind practicing law) because he doesn't want to do any one thing all the time. He loves variety, but no one will hire him for that. He needs to do many different things to earn his living and he also needs time for fun and travel. (Keep reading to see how many choices Alan has.)

Do any of these people sound like you? Well, here's a taste of what you're going to learn in the pages ahead.

YOU CAN FREELANCE JUST ABOUT ANYTHING

Accounting or law, teaching ancient history, even surgery. If you've got a profession you don't want to leave, but you wish you had more time or could do something else, that's important information to have. (I know people who are freelance lawyers at firms for which they used to work 80-plus hours a week.)

YOU CAN COACH ANYTHING

It's possible to coach people at anything. If you have a skill and enjoy helping others learn it, you can coach it. I personally know of a memoirs coach, a charisma coach and a performance anxiety coach, as well as a writing coach, a "caring for newborns" parenting coach, a dinner-party coach, a home decorating coach, an organizing coach and a home business coach (see "C" for Coaching).

You don't have to leave the house to do most coaching. Typically, coaches work with their clients on the telephone. Some use email. Others meet with their clients in person. The dinner party coach mentioned above does all three—she supports each step on the telephone, helps with invitations and online purchases via email and accompanies her clients to decorating shops, to markets and into their own kitchens.

YOU CAN BE SOUGHT OUT (AND PAID) AS AN EXPERT OR AUTHORITY

You can become an expert or an authority on anything you know how to do. Bone up from books on your subject and go looking on the internet for relevant websites or discussion groups so you can fill in any gaps in your knowledge. Don't assume you need a PhD. Look closer to home to find your expertise. You're already knowledgeable in a number of areas and the ones you like the best can be developed into authoritative status.

What's the difference between an expert and a coach? You can easily do both, but an expert also publishes books and newsletters, speaks, consults, teaches classes and often has a website with a bulletin board where he or she answers questions. My friend Gustav, a brilliant chef originally from Czechoslovakia who cooks at the best restaurants on the Greek island of Corfu, has decided to supplement his income and keep from getting bored during the winter months by setting up a website of his own on which he will give advice, share cooking secrets and sell some of his recipes. For example, someone wanted to know why meat didn't get tender in a stew no matter how long he cooked it. Gustav's secret: marinate it in pineapple juice! (He insists he got goat meat ready for grilling that way! I haven't tried it but I believe him.) Call that what you like. I call it a Food Coach.

YOU CAN BE AN AGENT OR A BROKER

If you'd rather learn from an expert than be one, but you long to share your learning experiences with others, you don't have to buy a school or build a spa. You can take your treasured teachers into someone else's school or spa! That way you can attend any class that interests you, and if the teacher is really first-rate, you can help get him or her paid work somewhere and take a small percentage for yourself. Win-win-win is what that might be called.

YOU CAN DO MORE THINGS ON THE ROAD THAN YOU EVER IMAGINED

If your town doesn't provide you with opportunities to share your gifts, how about taking them elsewhere? You can be an itinerant director of children's theater. Or a color consultant who visits towns twice a year. You just need one adoring fan in each town to set up the event and fill it with people from your mailing list of customers. How about traveling around your own town to different neighborhoods as a barber for children? Or a traveling dog groomer? Or a courier? You can make deliveries within 100 miles and charge less than FedEx or UPS—or you can charge more because you have some kind of specialty—say, transporting kids or pets or groceries or money or letters that need to be delivered by hand, or being great at last-minute, Sunday or all-night pickups and deliveries, like Elise, who you've already read about.

YOU CAN MAKE GOOD MONEY DOING THINGS FOR HOME BUSINESSES (OR LOCAL SMALL BUSINESSES) THAT THEY CAN'T DO FOR THEMSELVES

You can put on promotional events or decorate their windows with removable spray paint for the holidays. You can suggest (and run) a small booth outside their front door. You can make a short video for their local TV station—and broker the commercial, too. Or come up with an idea that will get them invited to be a guest on a show. You can put out a newsletter for them or design and deliver flyers or write press releases or feature stories about the business for the local paper. You can create great windows for them (and advertise your window-dressing skills at the same time by creating real interest.)

YOU CAN FANTASIZE AN IDEAL JOB DESCRIPTION AND CREATE THAT CAREER

If you love swimming and talking and you like to sleep all afternoon and go dancing in the evenings, you can invent a career that includes all of those activities and pursue it. That's how the most original careers are devised. In the case above, this person could have a speaking career (a lecturer or trainer) or a swimming career (a teacher or swimming pool salesperson to institutions) or both (a lecturer on the history of competitive swimming for the Olympics), and do it in Spain where they have siestas. Try it out yourself. Come up with the perfect job description and see if you have any bright ideas for inventing a career based on that description.

AND YOU CAN DO ALMOST ANYTHING YOU LOVE WITHOUT LOTS OF MONEY. HONEST.

Yes, you can travel the world or have a philanthropy or perform in your own plays or design and sell your own line of women's clothing—you name it— without much money at all. Everyone thinks you need a fortune to do such things, but the truth is, you'll do much better without it. (See "M" for Money if you don't believe me. And check out "F" for Fashion Designer or "T" for Travel. I've got stories of real people to back me up.)

So if you think you don't have a clue about what you really want, start reading. When the blizzard of ideas surrounds you with dozens of delightful possibilities you've never thought of before, I think you're going to change your mind.

HOW TO USE THIS BOOK

You can read the pages in this book in any order. It won't do you the slightest harm to open it in the middle and start there. You can also read from the beginning to the end. On each page you'll find what I think are interesting and useful ideas I've gotten from doing sessions with people or from letters and posts on my bulletin board, from Idea Parties I run as part of my workshops or just fun ideas that popped up in my brain when I thought I wasn't thinking.

Ideas are an entertaining read on their own, but you can't just skim over them. An idea is a special kind of creature. You have to dance with it, see how it moves, discover what it wakes up inside you.

Thinking is not a spectator sport. There is no end to ideas, but to select out the ones that are relevant for your life or to allow them to stimulate ideas in your own head, you must let them have an impact on you. Your response to an idea is a crucial part of the process. If you combine the ideas on these pages and your own responses, you can create a fresh and exciting future for yourself—one you never imagined was possible.

If you're not usually an "idea person," this can turn you into one. If you are, you might think that you already have too many ideas; but the pages that follow will help you select the ones that are right for you and give you strategies that can make them real, no matter what the present realities of your life may be.

So resist the impulse to do a little reading first. Pick up a pen or pencil and keep it near you before you read another page. Here's what to do with an idea:

1) Dog-ear the pages with the most interesting ideas on them. I do it on the lower part of the page. I also dog-ear the upper part to mark where I left off reading. Some people can't bear to fold a page and for them I suggest you go to the back inside cover of this book. I've left it blank, so you can write the page numbers there.

2) Write a note on the page about what part of this idea is interesting to you and why. Don't neglect to do this or you might not understand later what flashed in your mind and these mind-flashes are incredibly valuable messages from the most creative part of your brain.

3) Apply the "Idea Soup" technique, which can be found in Appendix 2 at the end of the book.

(Of course, if you find an idea so great you absolutely have to do it now, that's different. Go straight to step 3 and get rolling!)

The underlying goal of this book is to get you to be an idea person. You don't have to DO every one of the plans you come up with, but you do have to THINK about them, to look out a window or draw on a napkin and think them through the process the best you can. Try to imagine actual steps—what you'd be doing during your work day, how you'd bring in customers. See if you can put yourself into an imaginary scene where you're delivering your service or product to them. Where would you be? Then think about how many days a week you'd want for yourself, away from your imaginary business. Such imaginings are incredibly helpful and if you don't usually do them automatically, you should pick up the practice right now. There are some very good reasons for it.

First of all, this will help you to become a good thinker. Second, you'll be doing the kind of rehearsal that will give you confidence when the time comes for you to step forward and take action. Thinking about every idea here that's even remotely interesting is time well spent because, without the confidence you'll gain, you might hesitate forever. You'll imagine monsters that don't exist (and be unprepared for some that do!) unless you sit back and say to yourself, "Suppose I actually did this one. What would I do first? What would I need? Who can help me find this information?"

That's the first step towards action. In fact, it *is* action. Real action. Don't pass up the chance to work out some ideas as you read through the following pages.

Keep this book with you and open it when you're stuck in traffic (or on a long plane flight or in a line) and I promise you'll get the full benefit—just as long as you have something to write with at hand. It's essential to catch your own thoughts. Don't let them fly away. They could prove more valuable to you than anything I could possibly put on these pages.

PART ONE: IDEA WARM UP

The purpose of this section is to give you a warm-up for the ideas that follow. For the next few pages I'll be tossing ideas at you as fast as they come just to loosen you up and give you a notion of the richness and variety of what's available—and to get your mind up to creative thinking speed. The flurry of ideas in this first part is like a snowstorm, or, more accurately, a "Form-storm". The ideas come too fast to be examined and they zigzag in unexpected ways. That's deliberate. A Form-storm is designed to get you away from habitual thinking so you can expand the narrow focus you might have to the rich variety of forms your work life can take. In the main part of this book, IDEAS, you'll be asked to slow down again and do some thinking about almost every idea, but by then I predict you'll already be thinking differently.

So let's talk first about self-employment. Before you start assuming that working for yourself is too insecure or you can't make decent money at it or you have to find a location and buy lots of office furniture—or that it takes a huge effort or inside connections, or expensive advertising to get paying customers—take a look at Mindy's story. Mindy loved photography but worked as an administrative assistant. After getting laid off from her job, Mindy started teaching photography in her home just to pay the rent until she could find another job. (See "H" for Home Businesses).

The problem was, she didn't have a darkroom. But she did have a secret weapon (one I hope you'll create for yourself before you're finished with this book) called a Success Team. That's a group of friends who meet regularly to help each other achieve dreams. (See Appendix 4: Support Systems.)

Mindy's Success Team suggested she teach photography classes on "How to See," which is exactly what she did, using photos and slides, handing out cardboard frames for her students to look through as they walked through their daily life. To her surprise, she did very well at these classes because she really had a flare for teaching her subject and had many happy students. Her classes began to grow in no time by word of mouth.

Where did she get paying students in the first place? Her teammates went through their address books, called their friends and promoted her class. Two of them became students themselves. Her first class filled up within a week. ("A full class is one that brings in enough money to pay my rent that month," Mindy explained.)

Mindy could have built that little source of income into an profit-creating business by starting a lecture series on the same subject at an existing adult education group like The Learning Annex, or on a telephone conference call while her students viewed sample photos on their computers. She could have easily made an audio or video recording of every class and turned it into a taped course, using a CD-ROM for the photos she wanted to discuss—and then sold them all on her website.

But how would she get the word out to the world when there's so much competition? Mindy, fortunately, didn't try thinking like a major corporation because she doesn't have to get the whole world to come to her site, only the people who already know her and the people they refer, all on her email mailing list (to which she could send notices of any kind in a single moment, no expensive printing or licking stamps required).

Mindy's teaching website could have had a bulletin board on which she answered questions, building her reputation as an expert. She could have eventually used these already-written exchanges to create her own book of tips at almost no cost to her as a simplified *"e-book"* and made it available right on her website. And she could have and gotten paid for her e-book in advance on the computer as well. Or she could have turned her ideas into a "real" book—that is, published and made into a hard copy using a revolutionary advance in book publishing called Print On Demand, a computerized way to create professional-looking books one at a time—instead of paying out thousands of dollars and ending up with a garage full of books you have to sell. Where would she do that? There are many reputable companies offering very low-cost publishing to anyone who wants to have their book in print. (See the ads in "Writers Digest Magazine" or do a search for "Self Publishing" on the internet.)

With a book, she'd have a much easier time getting invitations to be a motivational speaker on the lucrative lecture circuit. Motivational? Yes, she wouldn't have to limit herself to amateur photographers. They don't pay much anyway. She'd be much better off speaking to groups with no special focus, groups of all kinds from the Rotary Clubs to garden clubs about "How to Wake Up Your Eyes" (to the beauty of this world, or to find your own personal vision, or a dozen other topics) regardless of whether they're interested in photography or not.

Have I gotten your attention? Or do you think most of these ideas are simply pie-in-the-sky? If you do, you'd better head over to my website (*www.barbarasher.com*) and read my bio. I do everything I've just described above rather successfully, and have for years—on my own, from my home, with one part-time assistant and no bank loans. (Yes, I do have a literary agent and a publishing house for many of my books, but I don't suggest that route anywhere in these pages. You can't control getting published by a major house, but you have a lot of control over every idea above.)

Mindy might have built her teaching business until it brought in much more than the bare minimum she needed for rent, but another business presented itself and now Mindy is on her way to having enough money to buy her own apartment. Here's what happened:

At lunch one day a friend complained about getting no responses to having her photo online with one of the internet dating services. Mindy saw the photo she was using and knew she needed a better one, so they set up a date and took some pictures. A day or two later the friend posted her new photo on the dating site and got 45 responses.

Friends lined up for photos so Mindy threw parties and took photos of them all. They all got similar results. A few of them called the newspapers and soon Mindy appeared in several major New York papers, and a few weeks later on CNN!

These days she gets paid for taking photos of singles to use on internet dating sites—and she's doing very well because she's got a gift for catching something special in every photo she takes. Her pictures get results. Now she has a waiting list of people who want their photos taken and she's being courted by three different internet dating services to work for them exclusively. The last time I talked to Mindy, she had hired two assistants, and brings in five times the money she earned while working for someone else. If you want to see her work, go to her website (*www.singleshots.com*) or come to mine! I was so impressed with the before and after photos on Mindy's original homemade website, I got her to take my photo before she got too famous to have time for me!

Is self-employment starting to look more interesting?

Mindy's got the kind of business that doesn't require much investment. She has no inventory and doesn't rent a store. She doesn't manufacture a product, either. Mindy's in what's called a "service business". The range of service businesses you can start without much trouble is dizzying. So read about all the variations below, and when you're done, you just might want to put this book down and take a long walk to re-think your notions about what's available in this world.

I started out totally broke, so I like service businesses. You don't need to buy or manufacture or store or ship anything, and you don't need to sit in a store all day trying to sell enough to pay the rent. Nothing is less expensive regarding overhead, especially now that the internet has come along to help us send out free announcements. If you don't have a dime and you do have a skill or two (as everyone does), try a service business.

Here's a small sample of some alternative forms a service business might take that you might not have thought of.

You can run your business at unexpected locations.

"I'll be retiring soon, and I would love to be a fix-it guy, you know, a handyman," someone said in a recent workshop I did in Jacksonville, Florida. "It would make me happy and bring in some income if I could be someone who repairs toasters, lamps, that kind of thing, but there are some real problems. For one thing, most people don't repair things anymore, they just throw them out and buy new ones."

That's a perfect example of a dream-smashing myth if I ever heard one, and I wondered where he got it. It turned out he got it from someone who sells to the upscale 18 to 38 year old market. My workshop had about two hundred people in the audience and most of them were over 40.

"How many of you would rather repair your broken stuff than buy new stuff?" About 190 hands went up.

He was surprised and impressed, but then he got concerned.

"You should all know I don't know how to do everything, like computers or furnaces or that sort of thing, and I really don't want to learn how, either."

"How about finding people who are good at those other things?" I suggested. "Ask them in to repair your computer and your furnace, or anything you don't know how to repair yourself, until you find the highest quality people, and then act as an agent for them." (See "A" for Agent.) "That means that you go out and get every kind of repair business and if you can't do it, you call them. It would be worth the 15% or 20% you'd take as a commission for them to get extra work, and you should be able to charge good rates for reliable, capable people."

"Wow!" he said. "I never thought of that. How would I get people to call me to fix things? Is everyone in this room actually going to give me a toaster to repair?"

"Oh, I think many of them would call you if you handed out a card," I laughed. "But I bet you didn't bring one, right?" He hadn't. "Then I advise you to borrow a few sheets of paper and ask them all for their telephone numbers, mailing addresses or email addresses and start your mailing list."

"And I bet many of them would come to a class to learn how to fix a toaster or a lamp. And most of them, once they learned how, would call you in to do the work anyway." I turned to the audience and asked, them. "Am I right?"

They laughed and agreed.

"You could give the classes for free, or almost free, in your own workroom at home. But you can also give classes at a community center, or even better, you could offer classes at a hardware store. The owner might be very happy to advertise and bring in people for your class as a way of bringing in new customers. Especially since you'd be teaching them something that might require them to purchase parts from the store. Also, most hardware stores get requests for repair work and they might be happy to send it your way."

"Wow," he said again. I sent him around the room to get the names and telephone numbers of people who would be interested in attending his first class. One raised her hand and said, "My uncle has a hardware store. Do you want me to talk to him?"

That's an Idea Party for you.

Think about the stores you go to most often and think about something related to that store that you'd enjoy teaching. You might want to consider teaching on their premises like he plans to do.

After the workshop he said, "I thought I was a good idea person, but you just shot those ideas out like popcorn!"

"I bet you are a good idea person," I said, "but you got stuck behind the myth that nobody wants your skills anymore so you stopped yourself before you got started. That's one of the best reasons to run our ideas past other people. Nothing beats having a whole room full of people to spot those myths and come up with ideas that dissolve them."

He's a believer now, and he can run an Idea Party anytime he needs some more ideas. (So can you. See Appendix 3: Idea Parties.) I love Idea Parties. They're responsible for making more impossible dreams come true than anything I know of.

NOTE: If you want to participate in any of the telephone Idea Parties I often run, be sure to get on my mailing list! Just go to *www.barbarasher.com*, click on "Mailing List" and sign up. Don't worry, I won't fill up your mailbox. I don't send out lots of email, but when I do, it's something you'll want to know about.

Working out of your home can be an excellent, low-risk way to start a business without a lot of expense or risk. Another person at the same workshop stood up to tell us his wish and his obstacle.

"I love to cook," he said, "but my dad had a restaurant and I never want those headaches."

"How about a dinner club?" I suggested. "How about a dinner club for singles, in fact? Upscale singles, who'd be willing to pay a decent amount to meet other upscale singles. If you have a nice, well-equipped kitchen, you can start a private dinner club with a minimum of licenses. If you don't have the right kind of home, pitch someone who does. That person might be happy to have the party at his or her home in order to be at all the parties!"

People started calling out from the audience. "Hey, I'm not single but I'd love to come to cooking classes held in someone's home." Other people called out, "So would I!" One woman said, "Can you teach me how to make sushi?" and the man who loved cooking said, "Sure! There's one fabulous fish store in this town. Oh," he paused. "I don't think they carry the fixings; the ingredients you get in Japanese food stores."

A voice from the back rang out. "Don't worry. I get all my sushi fixings, and cooking utensils too, from a catalog. I'll give you the name of it." And our restaurateur was off and running.

To see more ideas for running a business from home, go to "H" for Home businesses. You're also going to be reading about some great ideas for running your business more unusual locations. Here's a preview to whet your appetite.

Teach a craft in someone else's home to a group of friends.

I read about this in a magazine called "Time Out" a few months ago and loved the idea. Groups of friends would get together once a month or so and hire a craftsperson to come to one of their homes and teach them how to do something, such as quilting, needlepoint, lace-making, or watercolor painting. They had a wonderful time, and the artisan was paid for her time—about three hours—and often earned an additional profit from selling crafts materials she brought with her.

That's a nice idea for a hostess, but it's a *great* idea for a craftsperson.

The significant element in this form isn't really the location—although the rent-free aspect is a revelation to people who always fret about where to hold a class and how much it will cost, and this is especially lovely because it reduces your overhead to almost nothing—it's the fact that someone gets a group of customers together and pays you to do something for them. Again, look at the savings: you don't have to advertise or promote the class to bring in people. The host will do it for you.

Why not put on a play? Or have a reading? You might bring the audience into the cast by giving them a short rehearsal and letting them read from a script. You could start in the afternoon and go into the evening when guests would arrive to see the reading and have an actual performance. You can even start an ongoing amateur theater group for them and teach them how to run it. Or have them bring you in as the director or acting teacher. You could have your "cast" bring their own costumes! Or learn how to create them from clothes in their attics or local thrift stores. Or start a group business sewing costumes for the theater or for local school productions.

If you love the costumes more than the acting or directing, forget the theater entirely and teach your class how to sew costumes for their children at Halloween or for costume parties, or how to make dolls, or how to turn their own clothes that don't fit into perfectly tailored fashion statements. (You'll get lots of business from people who would rather you did the work for them, once they see how hard it is. And how good you are. See "S" for Stitcher.)

What kind of qualifications do you need? Well, you have to be good at what you do, and good at teaching it, or you won't be invited back. But that's it. No applications or tests have to be taken, and your credentials can be solely your ability to teach something they'd like to learn. Many people living in suburbs hesitate to leave home at night to go to classes in nearby cities, but are yearning for interesting ways to get together with their friends.

What if you expand the venue from other people's living rooms to other people's workrooms or backyards or kitchens or garages? With those spaces available to you and the audience provided by the sponsor of the party, you could teach cooking, pottery-making, gardening, auto-maintenance, home repair or carpentry. Teach these classes to uncharacteristic groups of people like women or retirees or kids at risk and you'll probably have good luck at getting free publicity, too, because teaching people who need but can't afford your services is both interesting and newsworthy, and it feels good to readers. Newspapers are always looking for such stories.

(Notice how we've slipped from what you'll do to how you'll market it? That's how ideas work. Don't rein them in. Watch what happens if they run wherever they want to.)

Back to the notion of teaching a group of friends in their homes: another idea that appeals to me is doing an ongoing series—for example, a career series in people's homes. You can gather information about jobs and create support teams to help them go looking. Or you can simply talk about what's available. For that matter, you can teach them how to start their own home businesses, and if they opt for that, you can become their beginning business coach, meeting with them three times a month on the telephone to help them solve problems and keep moving. (If you don't know about some of the businesses they want to start, you can find someone who does and be an agency that refers coaches. Think of all the coaches you could have in your stable! If this appeals to you, head over to "C" for Coaching and look at the list of ideas for things that can be coached.)

You can also teach a language and culture series, like how to speak Italian. Imagine getting together once a week with a group of eight people, cooking up a great Italian meal and eating it together, all the while speaking only Italian (with your help, of course). You might even consider getting them ready for a trip to Italy. A local travel agent would love you for that, and not only give you some kind of incentive (like free travel) but use some of their budget to advertise your class for you.

If you're like most of us, the idea of working in other people's homes—or even other people's stores—is a new one and deserves a little time to mull over. So let's take a moment for you to think about it. Pick up your pencil and see if you can think of some other unexpected venues where someone could provide a service and earn money. The following exercise might stimulate your thinking.

MAKE A LIST

Imagine you're in a situation where you need $2,000 and you have to come up with ten ways to earn money—and each must take place in a different location. To make it worth your while, pretend each idea will bring you $200.

1. _____
2. _____
3. _____
4. _____
5. _____
6. _____
7. _____
8. _____
9. _____
10. _____

If you didn't come up with 10 ways to earn your $2,000 call your friends or email some buddies—or come on my bulletin board at www.barbarasher.com and ask for more ideas. Asking for ideas will be good practice for you!

Here's another idea that doesn't really have a specific venue. You can do it from home, of course, but many colleges have students who do this for their schools: You can be a booking agent and bring shows or bands (or even circuses) to your town. It's a fun job if you don't like to travel but do like to see and hang out with interesting performers. I have a friend who lives with his wife in the Catskills and brings classical musicians as well as rock bands to his small town and gets a great turnout.

Or you can be a talent agent and have your own stable of good speakers or performers and booking agents will call you (see "A" for Agent).

Often local people or businesses interested in the betterment of their towns will be willing to pay for your services and sponsor the event you're producing as well. Check with your local Chamber of Commerce and tell them what you'd like to do. Start with nearby towns you can find on the internet. If they have a website, they may be forward-thinking. (Of course, if they don't have a website, maybe you should contact them and offer to create one for them!)

Let's talk about teaching

Don't get locked in by visions of school buildings, lesson plans and too many hours of administrative tasks. Teaching is the most portable skill of all. (A few others are nursing, administrative assistant with language skills, librarian, cook, seamstress or nanny.) You can teach what you know, and you can teach what you wish you knew. If you're a natural teacher, you can teach anything at all. You can be a speaker or a corporate trainer or an online tutor if you have teaching skills.

You can teach a huge range of subjects—in people's homes as we mentioned before, but also in community colleges, adult education groups or on the internet. You can teach things you haven't mastered by using someone else's book as a class guide. (I often get emails from people who use my books for that purpose. Some of them are college professors or career counselors. Others have no special credentials at all and are doing a very good job.) If there's a book that you feel would be valuable to people, you can teach it to a group of friends and learn about it at the same time.

You can teach dancing, writing, assertiveness training and computer skills. Yes, computer skills, even if you only know how to handle emails and surf the

40

net. Why would anyone want to learn from an amateur like you? Because they're intimidated by a pro and don't think it's even possible for them to learn anything about computers. Think about the "home party" form again and envision a group of friends, people who feel totally stupid about computers, whose kids and spouses are using computers every day and don't have the tact or patience to teach them. Shed your pre-conceptions about what it takes to be a computer teacher and imagine teaching them the way someone taught you to play guitar or drive a car, or to walk when you were a baby for that matter: in an informal, hands-on way, not once but a number of times until you got it. And think of how great your students would feel when they showed the rest of the family how to create a weblog or use a newsgroup or Instant Messaging. How can you resist?

Now, if you'd love to *learn* something but don't want to go back to school, you can hire a teacher. Just for you. I know a number of people who have done it with fantastic results. Where did they find them? Bill took a one-day class in writing for TV sit-coms and liked the teacher so much he called and offered him $200 for a two-hour phone session each week. (Those sessions helped him produce several screenplays which he is now shopping around to the studios.) My assistant, Andrea, met a young, award-winning playwright and hired her to teach a two-semester writing course in her home for a group of Andrea's friends. (Lots of talented people need money. And lots of them love to teach.)

You can work at home

You can use your computer to sell your hand-crafted jewelry or your used books about mountain climbing. You can be a virtual assistant and help someone with their bills, insurance, and airline tickets. You can write letters from a transcriber or take telephone messages for salespeople on the road.

While you have to be careful of scams when you see offers to "Make Big Bucks From Your Home" licking envelopes, there are many cottage industries that are completely legitimate. In *The Work At Home Sourcebook* by Lynie Arden, I saw companies I've ordered from in the past like Country Curtains, Inc. and Dainty Maid Manufacturing Company, both offering work to people who sew, or "stitchers" as they're often called. There are knitting opportunities, too.

I did notice that a company that outsourced embroidering has dwindled to only one worker at the time of the writing of this book and may have disappeared completely by now. Now an idea person might wonder if he or she couldn't start her own cottage industry and wake up some new markets for embroidery.

You can use your telephone to do more than make cold sales calls (something that would put me right in front of a TV set with a carton of chocolate ice cream and a big spoon in my hand.) For example, you can run telephone classes (I do) or email classes online. Or on a weblog (see "W" for Weblog).

And, of course, you can bring children (or pets or valuables for that matter) into your home to watch over while the owners are away. You could call that the "Haven model" of home business.

You can also work *from* home

You might do all your work out in the world as a gardener or a consultant, a speaker on the lecture circuit or flying to China, but the correspondence—the business telephone, the fax, email—all takes place in your home. That just means you're your own boss and you've got what's known as a Home Business. These days with the internet and other technology leveling the playing field, it's very possible for a small time operator to be self-employed and eat very well.

You can make things and sell them

That's called manufacturing, although that seems like a big word if you're making cookies or crafts. You can make things, and sell them too, in a way that won't put you in the poorhouse or leave you with a garage full of baskets or Victorian feathered hats…

The selling part is called "retail" (unless you sell to someone who will sell it again, in which case it's called "wholesale"). I don't love any of those words—or "service" either, to be honest—because they immediately take my imagination away from the loveable world of ideas where I can picture creative small-time operators doing interesting things and making enough money, and bump it over into the dreary world of Boring Business Terminology where everyone wants to get on the stock exchange and doesn't much care about the loveable stuff. I'm pretty sure such people won't see one idea in this book that's worth discussing, and anyway they use words like "scalable" and "pro forma". Never mind. They have their own books. But in case you read something besides this one book, you might need their terminology here and there.

There are ways to sell what you make (or what someone else makes) that do not require a shop of your own, or any shop at all, and won't send you begging for a loan at the local bank after spending months sweating out a business plan they won't laugh at.

With micro-businesses, when you make something, you often have to do the selling too. You may make dolls and offer them for sale at a booth in a craft fair, or on your website. You may collect antiques and sell them in an antique barn where you rent a small space among many other antique dealers. (This can be a nice option if you don't want to spend all your time at the "shop" because many dealers take turns watching each other's areas.) Sometimes you can sell your truly great fudge to a market or a restaurant or a caterer. (That makes you a "wholesaler" I guess. Doesn't really seem to work with fudge, does it? Unless, of course, you have a huge factory and hundreds of people on your fudge assembly line. You can already guess that the only assembly lines I like are the ones you set up in your kitchen with your family and some friends, where you play loud music and tell jokes.)

And you can sell gift baskets and flowers and kids' toys in the halls of a corporation to busy workers who don't have time to shop on their way home from work.

MAKE A LIST

I know I've left out dozens of places you can sell from. Go into your imagination (and your rolodex or email list to ask for other people's input) and see how many more locations you can find to showcase and sell an item you've made or bought. Write them down in the space below while your brain is warmed up, so you won't forget them:

_____

_____

_____

_____

_____

_____

_____

_____

(Incidentally, if you want to share any of your great ideas, send them to me and I'll put them in my next Idea Book. If I use your idea, I'll send you a copy as a "thank you"! Go to the back of this book to a page called "Write Me." I'd love to hear from you.)

But if you simply do not want to be self-employed, if you just want to show up, do your work and subsidize you dreams with the money you earn, I'm with you all the way. You don't have to invent and manage a company of your own. But you also don't have to sign up for a 52-week year with eight (or more) hours a day.

You don't need a full-time job to earn money. You can work as a temp or on a project-basis only.

You know what a temp is—you go to an agency and they farm you out, or you show up at the office of a lawyer you know and do paperwork three days a week. Contract work isn't as well known. That's a job which is tied to a project and can last for a few months. Contract work is popular in the information technology field, and also in TV or film production where they need people to work on projects and don't need them when the projects are completed.

Both temp and contract work will pay your bills and leave you time to do what you really love. Temp work gives you time to paint or be with your family or read, and contract work gives you time to travel to the Himalayas for a few months at a time. Just remember, you can find the kind of work that suits your dreams.

Remember, too, you don't have to do just one part-time job. It might be smarter and more interesting to do work at different part-time jobs to bring in money. Then if one doesn't work out, you don't have that heart-stopping interim where you can't pay your rent.

You can have more than one source of income

Who said you had to find the one thing that will earn all the money you need? No wonder people get stuck. If none of the things you like to do will make enough money on their own to support you, don't reject them. Do them all. Create a number of profit centers or income streams, and if one or two don't work, the others will. Together, you can bring in whatever money you need without having to choose only one way to do it. There are lots of people who have been doing exactly this for years, and I'm one of them. I write books and do speaking engagements, I do individual consultations and make television specials for public TV. I teach on the phone and run Idea Parties on the phone as well. And I run workshops where I train coaches to use my techniques. I also sell audio sets. I love having a variety of income sources, but even more, I love never being bored by doing the same thing every day.

A woman who was the subject of one of my telephone classes wanted to work at home designing and sewing clothes. She gave away the fact that she's highly creative when she said, "Don't ask me to do something twice!" Every truly creative craftsperson I've ever met says the same thing. That means they have to find a way to do things once (or create a cottage industry to make many copies of their designs).

She really got my attention when she mentioned that her son requested a copy of the yellow zoot-suit Jim Carey wore in the film, "The Mask". That was one truly extreme suit and she had to create her own pattern, but all she said was, "Now that was fun!"

If she limited herself to sewing—and there's no need for her to do this because she could be a designer or consultant for a theater where other people could do the sewing—she could do any (or all) of the following:

1) Run ongoing classes every week or two, in which she teaches mothers how to sew their own Halloween costumes, for example. Classes could be held at the home of one student, attended by her friends. If each student paid $20 plus any materials they bought (let's say $25 altogether), and there were seven friends attending, she'd earn $175 for a 2–3 hour class. If she got some publicity, she could easily run two of these each week in the afternoons or evenings. That's about $350 each week.

2) She'd probably get commissions to sew some costumes herself if she brought samples of her work—or photographs of it—to her class. At $75–250 per costume, she could probably earn at least $500 per month.

3) She could teach "How to Throw A Successful Costume Party" in tandem with a friend who's good at parties, or teach another subject on the telephone. How could she teach sewing on the phone? Well, she could make and mail a workbook to every student so each person could look at the illustrations as she referred to them. Or, if her students had some kind of broadband access to the internet, she could hold her class on the computer screen while talking to students on the telephone. She could show them still photos or sketches of what they're supposed to be doing while giving instructions. Incidentally, with those photos or sketches, and a transcript of her telephone classes, she'd be creating something a lot like a printed crafts book, wouldn't she?

But how could she get it published? Or self-publish it without mortgaging the homestead?

Here's how: Get someone to burn the pictures and the voice on a CD (Who? I bet everyone you know has a friend or relative with a computer that can do that without much trouble at all.)

If she preferred a full video, she could produce a series of "shows" in her home and easily burn the whole thing onto a DVD. Then, her telephone students could play her DVD while they're on the phone with her and watch her actually sewing—that's like a TV crafts show. Of course, they could also see her "live" if she had a webcam and was on camera. That way students could ask questions she'd be able to answer on the spot and everyone could see exactly what she was doing. (I hope your mind is starting to spin a little bit as you realize you can also teach art that way, as well as engine repair or indoor gardening.)

With the teacher on camera and the students watching their computer screens while they listen to her on the telephone, it's a lot like a live class except the students can stay home and get into their pajamas if they like. And the time is already here that anyone can do a web radio broadcast too. Live. In the their own kitchen.

It won't be hard for her—or you—to get 10–20 people signing up for each class if you have a mailing list or can get a newspaper or national crafts magazine to write an article about you. These are very modest numbers. I usually get over 80 people each time I do a tele-class, but you can do quite well with five to ten people. And you can sell materials to your students in any of these teaching mediums to raise your income even more.

For example, each student might pay, say, $15 for this one-hour telephone class. If 20 people sign up, that's another $300. And anything done on the phone can easily be recorded and become an audiotape set for sale on your website. Or you can combine them on a CD, as I mentioned above.

4) She could introduce herself to dance clubs, like the Swing Dance Club which has its own contests and weekly dances at a nightclub near her. "Everyone is dying for some vintage 30's clothes to dance in," she said. The idea delighted her. She said she'd love to sew vintage costumes for swing dancers. And that's a very nifty idea and a very smart way to market her costume-making skills. (I advised her to sew her own label into each outfit with instructions on how to find her.)

You can pick up quick cash when you need it

I've got a rather jolly list of ways to do this (see "Q" for Quick Cash) but right now I just want to introduce the "quick cash" concept so you'll understand how many ways you can get money without a full time job. Quick cash can be for necessities, but it also comes in handy when you find a fabulous guitar you must have, or a course you must attend and you simply don't have the money or much time to get it. You can use the ideas in the Quick Cash chapter whether you're a happy beach bum or fully employed. It's just a bit extra for special things.

Or you can slowly accumulate a nest egg to finance your dreams

Just because you can't afford your dream now doesn't mean you can't afford it in a few years. If it's your dream to go back to school or to live on an island in the Aegean or to buy your own horse, you need a piggy bank of some kind and special activities that funnel money into it and nowhere else. This, like quick cash, can be done "on the side," without reference to how you earn your other income.

My point? Any dream can come true, whether you need extra money or extra time or just some brand-new way to do it.

That's what this book is for.

That was your Idea Warm Up. I hope you had some fun reading this section and enjoyed shaking loose some of that methodical thinking. Most of all, I hope you now can see that there are many, many ways to go after any dream—and that your dream is almost certainly within reach.

Now it's time to jump into the actual Idea Party that this book is intended to be. A book is just one of many kinds of Idea Parties, so when you're finished with the ideas inside be sure to go to "Appendix 3: Idea Parties" to learn how to run your own Idea Parties.

Got your pencil in your hand? Let's look at some ideas.

PART TWO

IDEAS A to Z

As promised, here are even more ideas—a lot more—for you to look at. They're in alphabetical order, but I have purposely not put each item in strict alphabetical order within each of the 26 lettered chapters. There's a reason for this: I want you to see as many unexpected ideas as possible while you're reading this book. That way you might stumble on something important in areas you haven't considered before.

Keep that pencil nearby and circle anything you like (note anything you dislike, too) and write your H-Level number next to that sentence in the margin. To refresh your memory, an H-Level of 10 is an idea, or part of one, that you absolutely love. An H-Level of 1 is something you definitely do not want in your life. Anything that earns an H-Level of 7 or above from you is significant. Anything under a 4 is equally significant. Don't spend too much time assigning the middle numbers. They can require too much head-scratching and aren't as relevant, so you don't have to think about them unless you've got a lot of time on your hands.

In the margins I've provided space for you to take notes and write comments. You'll do your best thinking if you jump in with your own reactions as often as you can. This is your future we're talking about, so don't be shy about writing anything important in it. (Of course, if you've borrowed it, just keep lots of blank paper nearby for your notes.)

A

Ancillary skills for your "good-enough job"

[an.cil.lar.y (adj) 1. in a position of lesser importance, 2. providing support for somebody or something.]

When we talk about your "good-enough job" we're not talking about your dream, just a source of income that will subsidize your dream. You can work at almost anything that doesn't make you sick, but it's a lot more pleasant to do something you're good at than something that bores you to death. You'll probably earn more money, too, because we always shine at things we like to do. If you like driving, researching, talking, fixing things or creating order, there's a good-enough job waiting for you. While using these ancillary skills may not be your dream, they're great for your good-enough job.

A client of mine loved writing fiction and was willing to work at a job to support it, but he just couldn't stand the job he had as a salesman.

"I'm not a salesman. I shouldn't be doing this," he said.

"What do you do at home when you're avoiding writing?" I asked.

He laughed. "I love to organize my house, to make sure there's a place for everything. I've come up with some really ingenious organizing systems. My accountant says I should rent out my receipts, they're so organized!"

"Well, that's that," I said. "You're a personal assistant and if I didn't already have one, I'd hire you myself. How much money do you need to earn each year?"

The amount wasn't overwhelming since he had some income from other sources.

"Great," I said. "Then you don't have to be a full-time personal assistant to a wealthy celebrity (they can be demanding). You can take five or ten clients and work half-days for each of them."

"Doing what?" he asked.

"Balancing their checkbooks, paying their bills, organizing their papers, creating systems to help them track expenses for their taxes, organizing their receipts, keeping track of their insurance, stuff like that." (For more, see "Assistant" below.)

"That would be fun!" he said.

"Not everyone would agree," I laughed.

"But who needs that service?"

"Who doesn't? Before you leave your job, offer to do it for one or two people you work with and get good recommendations. Next, try self-employed people, or busy professionals. You can even help other personal assistants! After all, you're an organizer. You could make sure their systems were up and running so they could be efficient. You could even train personal assistants and set up your own agency, except for one thing—and you don't want to forget this. You love to write. If there were two of you, one might own a personal assistant agency, and the other could have plenty of time to write, but you're just one person. So you might want to stick with a one-person service."

He chose the one-person service. You might want to choose the agency that specializes in people with your ancillary skills, whatever they are.

Now, stop for a moment here, at the beginning of this section, and think about what you've just read. Is there anything in that story that you find appealing? Look again, and if you find a word or a phrase that you liked, circle it lightly with a pencil. In the outside margin, write a number that represents how much you like it on a scale of one to ten (its "H-Level"). Take the time to do this at every moment while you're reading. The payoff for this little technique could be huge.

Then, if you really want to know who you are and what you want (and how to get it), if you're dead serious about wanting a life that will excite you and make you happy and still keep a roof over your head, take the time to answer the following questions:

1) What did you learn from writing H-Levels for this idea?
2) What elements of this idea might be useful for your dreams?
3) If you were going to pursue this idea—or help someone else pursue it— what steps would you take first?

These aren't just any old questions. Answering them requires that you practice three essential steps in goal achievement. First, you pay keen attention to anything that appeals to you, even if you don't yet understand its significance. That's like being a detective gathering clues. Second, you become curious about new methods of doing things and wonder how you might use them yourself. That step makes you creative and adaptable and confident. And third, you develop the habit of moving from thought to action.

That third step is the big one and can feel like a cliff instead of a step. Fear of moving from thought to action is what stops most people from achieving their dreams. That's not cowardice. No person in their right mind would consider jumping into action without having taken the first two steps. But after you become used to checking your H-Levels and you've developed a good eye for strategies, action stops feeling dangerous and becomes interesting. That change will transform your life. Guaranteed.

Assistant

At one time the only people with personal assistants were famous and rich, but now almost everyone can and should have one (including personal assistants!) Hiring a personal assistant doesn't have to be expensive if you have yours come in only once a week. An assistant can get all your bills ready to pay (and pay them for you, too), stay on the phone with tech support when your computer is having a bad day, be there for deliveries and send out FedEx's, order (and return) things you've bought from a catalog, make travel arrangements, maintain your website and/or take care of your car registration—whatever you need done. I believe that if everyone had a part-time personal assistant, they'd write more plays and design more gardens, have more fun and earn more money, too.

As a job, being a personal assistant is a very interesting choice: rather than sitting in a cubicle all day, you visit your different clients on different days. That gives you the flexibility to attend classes, go to movies in the daytime and work on any fun project that takes your fancy.

How to get started

You can post flyers in elevators or small stores in your area. If you'd like to be a "virtual assistant" you can operate from your home using your fax, phone and computer. Do a search on the internet for contract jobs or moonlighting. Last I looked there were sites offering the services of virtual assistants to potential employers. Take a look at InfoWord (*www.infoword.com*) to see what they offer and if that's the sort of thing that interests you. And be sure to take a look at one of the absolutely best sites on the internet, Craigslist (*www.craigslist.org*), where you can place a free classified ad offering your services.

Scheduler

If you like politics and have good organizing and administrative abilities you should consider being a scheduler. Who hires full-time schedulers? Famous, busy people, like your representatives and senators in the U.S. Congress, that's who. You can find out about this and other opportunities on Capitol Hill from a book called *How to Get a Job in Congress (Without Winning an Election)* by Christopher Porter.

Animals

If you love animals, you probably wish you could earn your living working with them. Well, you can. I've gathered a number of ideas in my travels, but if you want to see the vast range of possible careers with animals from some real professionals, check out the following:

- *105 Careers for Animal Lovers* and *The Companion Bird Lover's Guide to Careers* by Paula Fitzsimmons (contact: paula@pjpublications.com)

- *Career Success With Pets: How to Get Started, Get Going, Get Ahead... A complete guide to starting your own rewarding career with pets* by Kim Barber (Macmillan 1996)

Adventure guide for dogs

Someone on my bulletin board wrote that she was out walking in Golden Gate Park in San Francisco and watched a woman drive up in a truck filled with 7 or 8 big, happy, slobbery dogs. "She saw my big grin, handed me a business card that read 'Dawg Adventures' and told me that she takes people's dogs on these 'adventures' around the San Francisco Bay Area."

Does that sound like something you might be happy doing? I'm convinced that there's a special gene which real animal lovers possess, and they are only truly happy when they're near animals. If you're one of these uniquely gifted people, there are tons of ways you could be working with animals right now. You can find plenty of professional agencies on the web that can give you a taste of what it's like to take your love of animals and turn it into work. Visit *www.thepetstaff.com* to see what they do. (Go to *www.craigslist.org* for this one, too.)

Animal refuge

If you wish you had an animal refuge to help unwanted animals, don't assume you need to amass a fortune first to buy the land. Instead, you can join an existing refuge (I found sites for animal refuge centers in every part of North America as well as Tenerife, Venezuela and Kansai, Japan!); or locate people with land they're not using and ask them to donate it to your new foundation; or go out to the farm country closest to your home and find retired farmers who might be interested in helping, perhaps in return for some service they themselves need (lots of farmers do not want to sell their land, even when they're unable to use it themselves. Anyone who helps them hang on to it will go to heaven without question.) Or you can do what many people have done: start an animal refuge right now, in your home. Before you shrug off that last idea, think about these benefits:

1) You can start right away, and if you're an animal lover, you don't want animals in need to have to wait years for you to organize something big and ambitious: you want them to be safe right now, tonight.

2) You can learn the legal and/or non-profit ropes of animal refuges so that by the time you're ready for a Texas-sized spread for your animals, you'll know everything you need to know (and any legal or financial problems will have been on a very small scale).

3) You can fill that big heart of yours with something besides aching helplessness, because you'll be saving one or two or twelve fine creatures right now. It will give you the energy you need to keep moving until you get things exactly the way you want them.

Someone who did exactly that is Sandi Meinholz, director of Fine Feathered Friends Sanctuary, Inc. Sandi has created an aviary in her home. Check out her website (*www.feathered-friends.com*). You'll love it.

Portable Animal Grooming

If you have transportation and want to be your own boss, how about setting up a traveling Pet Washeteria? Well, you don't have to call it that, but you can be an animal groomer (if you've got a gift with animals) by setting up your grooming salon inside a van. If the weather is warm and you can do the grooming outdoors, all you need is a car or even a bike that pulls a cart, if you want to get a lot of attention (which translates as 'If you want to get a lot of free advertising.') Whatever you drive, make sure your name (and a great cartoon) are visibly painted on the outside of the vehicle.

You'll need to bring a galvanized bathtub, shampoo, combs, brushes, nail-cutters, teeth-cleaners, scissors, a blow dryer (plus a way to hook it up to electricity) and a portable platform with a harness setup to hold the creature still while you comb it. You might be a very welcome visitor to the homes of people who don't have time to take their pets in to be groomed, just don't want to do the job themselves, and especially dislike hair and water all over their homes.

Agent

Talent Agent

If you saw the film "Broadway Danny Rose" and would still like to handle talent, it's in your blood, and you'll do a great job. (See the movie again anyway, it's a gem!) Whether it be speakers, bands, presenters—these acts are all your product, they're what you're selling. If they get paid, you get paid. So, although finding work for your talent is all you're technically responsible for, you can also re-package, promote and market your acts. Help them dress better, line up singing coaches, send out press releases and create a hot brand for each one. Make your acts look good. Show that they've got something that's a hot commodity.

Clearly, the very first step is figuring out what you're booking: models, folksingers, look-alikes, motivational speakers. Once you've done that, get on the phone and figure out who's in charge of booking your people. Get to know the people who hire (in corporations, organizations, etc.) and the venues where your talent will show their stuff (hotels, event centers, small clubs). If you're booking models, your clients will be anyone in the fashion industry or in advertising agencies, of course, but models attract attention and are wanted for everything from store openings to walking around the floor of a boat show. If you're booking musical acts, all clubs and schools have someone who makes the decision as to who performs and when, but musical acts are also wanted by conferences and at corporate sales meetings. Get on the phone, call hotel sales or banquet offices or convention centers to contact event planners in different companies. Befriend event planners. Do favors if need be. Work for free. Show them what you've got.

Here's an interesting title that could give you all the detailed information you need: *How To Be Your Own Booking Agent And Save Thousands Of Dollars: A Performing Artist's Guide to a Successful Touring Career* by Jeri Goldstein. I haven't read it but the table of contents is impressive. It looks like she's done her homework. If you can learn to be your own booking agent from this book, you can learn how to do it for others, too.

Agents aren't only for performers, however. Sometimes the best way to get involved in what you love is to act as an agent and find work for someone you admire.

Agent for Health & Wellness Practitioners

Did you ever wish you could have a wellness spa and bring in all the fabulous teachers and healers you've worked with? Well, before you give up on that idea because you don't have the money to build a spa (and let me mention that if you don't already know how to run that kind of business you might not enjoy it once you did) think about this:

If the part you love most about this dream is working with gifted healers, and the longing that drives this dream is to bring their gifts to others—and maybe just a bit of recognition for having such good taste and such a good heart—then you should consider becoming an agent for healers instead of a spa owner.

As an agent you'd continue to seek and find exceptionally talented people in the fields that are important to you—from yoga to dance therapy—and help to place them in top spas around the country and the world. Many of them are not recognized widely and most are underpaid. You could help them, help the people who would discover them due to your efforts, and help yourself by taking a percentage of their fee for finding them work. You'd also enjoy seeking out new, talented people and whatever you paid for taking their classes would be tax deductible! That's a triple Win-Win-Win all around.

(If you're interested in bringing shows to your town, see "B" for Booking Agent.)

Artist

Yes, you can make a living as an artist. You can do the kind of art that people pay money for (designing fabrics, layout for ads, decorating) or you can teach art full-time—or as one of your many income streams (see "M" for Money)—or you can make art, have a show and sell lots of it and become the art world's darling and get really, really rich. I don't know how you do that last one but the people who do it appear to be insiders, so if that's the one you want, head for the art world and get to know everybody. If you just want the excitement of making the best art you can without worrying about whether or not it's saleable, and to find a good-enough source of income to keep you from starving to death, you'll have a very fine life. From everything I know about artists, they really know how to be happy if they're just allowed to do their art.

How does an artist become well known? Here's some good advice from working artists:

1) Keep turning out good work. Maintain the highest quality you're capable of.

2) Find a special subject or a niche that identifies you, like a brand. People who want your work (and reviewers who want to write about it) will be able to find you more easily that way.

3) Don't isolate yourself. Hang out with other artists, especially those whose work is similar or in some way related to yours, and when you hear of opportunities be sure to share your information. (Select the nicest, least competitive people to share with, incidentally. You'll find that they're the ones who will return the favor whenever they can.)

4) Find a way to show your best work as often as you can. Don't disappear from the scene. If galleries won't accept you, have your show in restaurants, schools, or in the home of a fan who is willing to have an open house on Saturdays or Sundays.

5) Get a copy of one of the Artist's Marketplace-type books and read a little every day. Before you select the book you want to own, look through them all in your local library or bookstore. Then choose the one that works best for you. (Don't worry too much about your choice. You can always go back and read the others as well!) These look useful: *Artist's Market & Graphic Designer's Market, 2004* by Mary Cox, *The*

Artist's Guide to New Markets: Opportunities to Show and Sell Art Beyond Galleries by Peggy Hadden and *The Business of Being an Artist* by Daniel Grant. (I've seen an out of date title that looks so useful, but no up-to-date editions and that is *The 1982-1983 National Directory of Shops, Galleries, Shows and Fairs* by Sally Ann Davis (Editor). You might try to find it online at a used book store. (Do a search for 'used books'. I found *abebooks.com, powells.com, alibris.com* and *addall.com* —and there are many more to choose from. I've used most of them myself, with great success.)

6) Never fail to put announcements of anything you do in the calendar/ events section of your local newspaper.

7) Speak in front of groups. Local organizations that meet on a regular basis (like garden clubs, investment conferences and service organizations like the Lions or Rotary Clubs, etc.) are always looking for interesting speakers. Offer to talk about some aspect of art that might interest them, like "Understanding Today's Art" or "Collecting Contemporary Art" or anything you think will draw an audience. If you have a slide show prepared, speaking can be easy. (You stand in the dark with a microphone and can read from your notes just like the academics do!) Best of all, you can use many of your own paintings to illustrate your points. (Don't forget to collect an email list at every appearance! A mailing list is worth many times its weight in gold. If you build one you'll easily be able to contact interested people about your next events.)

And thanks for being an artist. The world needs you.

Actor

Misc. acting jobs

Everyone says actors can't make money, but I've heard differently. Here are some fun jobs that can bring in some extra income for an actor:

"I taught in a course—at the University of Pittsburgh Medical School—where actors learned to play patients. The idea was to train medical students a bit before they went out and actually treated real patients."

But this type of course is now being taught all over the country. So, if you'd like to teach others to simulate patients (a.k.a. patient simulators), you may want to contact your local medical school. Alternatively, if you'd like to do the impersonating yourself, you should contact the medical school and see if there is someone who is coordinating the course. It is usually called "medical interviewing" and it might be a good income source. Here's another one:

"In our newspaper this week it was reported that people giving dinner parties are hiring actors/ amateurs to attend, dress and behave as normal guests. Their job is to have an argument or lover's tiff part way through the night, or behave obnoxiously to some of the other guests. This is supposed to spice up the dinner party and make it more memorable. Just when you think you've heard everything..."

B

Banquet Waiter

Banquet waiting is not at all the same as waiting tables in a restaurant. Surely you've seen waiters at weddings and big events wearing tuxedos and passing hors d'oeuvres. Those are banquet waiters. What they do is provide excellent service. They carry trays of food and serve from the left. They know how to pick up food with two forks in one hand. They can pour wine beautifully, make an art of folding napkins, and have the graciousness to make the customer feel they're getting their money's worth. Who hires banquet waiters? Caterers. Look in your yellow pages to find them. The big caterers all advertise so you can call to see if they hire waiters. It's usually good money, too.

If you'd like to find work out of town so you can also work on your novel, call some small resorts outside of your city. You can be a banquet waiter in the mountains or by the sea. You'll be on duty for every meal, but you'll have hours off without lots of phone calls in between setups and clean-offs to be by yourself and do your own work in a beautiful setting. I know someone who sublets her New York apartment for the whole summer and works in a Catskills resort where she lives for free. By the end of the summer she has an extra $4000 in her bank account.

(Don't forget to circle anything you like and write its H-Level in the margin. And don't forget to answer the questions What did you learn? What can you use for your own dream? How would you proceed? Okay, I'm going to trust you from now on. Don't let yourself down.)

Bed and Breakfast

Have you ever dreamed of having a little place in the country (or a big one), where you could offer grateful guests a unique, cozy getaway? That's exactly what Bed and Breakfasts are, and they range from simple accommodation to fancy havens full of antiques and cultural goings-on. Sounds like a great dream for someone with a lot of money, doesn't it? Well, don't cross it off just yet. Here's an idea that actually worked for someone who didn't have an extra dime.

Jan and her husband found a B&B in the countryside about 45 minutes from their home and after a few visits became friends with the owners. They learned that the owners had been in the business for 12 years and wished they could get away occasionally to do a little traveling themselves. Jan and her husband started giving them a hand on their free weekends, and after a while (once real trust had been established) arranged for them to get away for a whole week. This was the test they needed to see if they actually enjoyed doing the work and having all the responsibility instead of merely helping. They loved it. So, they made the couple an offer to become partners. The owners could travel half the year while Jan and her husband took over. Now the owners spend the winter months in Florida while Jan and Billy buy into the partnership with "sweat equity" (that is, they aren't paid a salary for their work), live rent-free, and send the owners half of the profits after expenses. When the owners return, Jan and Billy live in a small apartment on the premises and help out, or do some traveling too.

Did you love anything about this story? What other dream could you make come true this way? How would you put this idea into action for yourself?

Beach Bum

If you're someone who cares more about the quality of your life day to day than long-term goals or status in society, if spending your days and nights by the ocean makes you feel that life is worth living, you can find many ways to earn money to support yourself. I've met people who do boat detailing (that means cleaning up the boats while they're in dock), and I even heard of one amateur scuba diver who makes a steady income at the marina scraping barnacles off the hulls of the sailboats.

If you like to sail and you know how to cook, you can sign on to an ocean voyage as a chef (see "C" for Cooking). And, of course, you can be a very comfortable beach bum if you manage to make money on your computer as the "day traders" used to do when the stock market was at its hottest.

The point is, if you need to live by the sea, you can find ways to do it. It's simpler than it looks. You can be an electrician or a carpenter or handyman. Don't worry about losing your status as a Beach Bum if you're doing any of those perfectly respectable things. Your family will still call you a beach bum. I promise

Book lover for hire

You wouldn't think a book lover could build a career around her passion, but I know it's very possible. I love this story. It's about someone who insisted she didn't know what she wanted, but of course, like everyone, she did. She was sure she couldn't think of a thing she loved until I threw some random choices at her: Do you love athletics? Are you creative? Do you like books?

"Books! I love them!" she said.

"That's more like it! What kind?"

"Any kind. I just love turning people on to books."

Her friend walked up with a huge tome under her arm and said, "She's good at it too! Look at this book! I never would have picked it up. Now I can't put it down!"

"Why didn't you tell me you loved turning people on to books?" I asked.

"Because there's nothing you can do with it," she said.

"Really? How do you know that?"

"Well, I can't think of anything."

"I can," I said and started to run this list past her, just of what happened to occur to me that I know is possible:

1) Teach your skill to teachers and parents.

2) Get a small website with Tips on it—one of the students would probably set it up for free, or a grateful teacher could make it a class project. Become known as a resource and an expert.

3) Then you could send out a newsletter with recommendations for books. You might get publishers to advertise in your newsletter, or just pay you to do this because you are helping them sell books.

4) On your website you might have a bulletin board like I do, but design it for kids. They can tell you which books they're assigned and you can show them why those books are exciting. You might have a discussion area for teachers, too.

5) How to get paid? There are a lot of people who would like to know how you turn people on to books when they can't: teachers, parents, publishers. You can run classes on the telephone and let people pay to attend by sending you money via Paypal.

6) You can also ask your audiences to tell you what exactly you did that turned them on to books and figure out how to teach it. Then go on the lecture circuit. Talk to parents. Or to teachers. Credentials? Your website, your bulletin board, articles written about you.

7) Warm up at the local library until you're used to talking in front of people. ("Oh, I can do that already," she said!)

8) At an independent bookstore—maybe even a mega bookstore—you could have a regular speaking gig there like authors do, but you'll get people excited about someone else's books because that's what you love to do. You'll sell books for the bookstore and you'll get a lot of confidence about the value of what you're doing.

9) Have a little reading circle for your church or organization to help build your reputation and your mailing list. Especially your email list. You can

notify people where you'll be speaking and you can send them a bi-weekly recommendation.

10) You can speak in front of publishers and organizations that encourage reading clubs.

11) You could be a consultant to reading groups: put an ad in the paper that says, "Don't know what to read next? I'll visit your reading group and turn you on to great books."

12) You could find a school teacher friend of a friend and visit her classroom to turn the kids on to reading; maybe most of them wouldn't listen but two or three would probably weep with joy—"Is that good enough for you?" I asked. "Yes!!" she said.

13) You could develop a reputation through steady public relations. That means getting into local newspapers, clipping any articles written about you and creating a press kit to send to radio and TV shows.

14) You might get into national magazines when you're ready. (You can get into trade magazines and e-zines more easily and sooner.)

15) ...and then you could get on the lecture circuit and talk to parents' groups or teachers on how to make young people want to read, how to start the fire in them for reading; you could get a few advertisers and do a webcast on the internet, and call it "Irresistible Books": talk about your favorite book each week.

16) Finally, in some hospitals (and nearby libraries), doctors will hire a Bibliotherapist for depressed patients. The Bibliotherapist creates a list of

books for the patient to read to help them through their illness, or at least, cheer them up. If you find this idea intriguing you can read more about it in Salon Magazine. Here's the link:

www.salon.com/books/feature/2000/08/08/bibliotherapy

When I was through her mouth was open, so I said, "Am I making you crazy or do these look like useful ideas?" and she said, "My God, they're amazing— would you write them down? I had no idea!"

Now, take a look at that list again. If it's possible to create an income from the gift of making people love books, you can use the same methods to create income from anything you love at all. Give it some serious thought. What do you love to do that you were convinced couldn't make money? Can you rewrite this story and plug in what you love instead?

Finally, if you love reading books and need to earn some money and/or do some good, there are people hired by colleges to read books onto tapes or CDs for vision and learning impaired students. Look in the student employment office, where some jobs are made available to people not connected with the school.

Booking Agent

Colleges have budgets for bringing entertainment to the campus, and the students who take on the role of booking agent do the hiring. They find and hire bands, stand-up comics and motivational speakers to come to their campus. I've spoken to a few of them through the years, and all of them told me they intend to continue in the profession once they graduate, because it's so much fun. If you're a booking agent you've got the auditorium and you're looking for talent to fill it. Your job is to find and bring in ("book") people who will draw good audiences. It's a definite inside track for a groupie, but also for someone who likes to help discover talent. If you know of a good musical group or comedian who is still flying below the radar you can have a real influence on their success—a satisfying accomplishment for a true admirer of talent.

To track down the people you want to bring to your auditorium, look on the back of their CDs or in their latest book for contact information and call their agent. If they don't yet have an agent, call them personally. You'd be surprised who you'll find if you call information or check for phone numbers on the internet.

Business on a bike

Most people think the only business you can start with bicycles is a sales and repair business, but you can start a completely different kind of bike business and make a real splash. That's what Doug Woods of Boulder Bike Taxi did. He just started a short time ago and now his bikes and "drivers" are carting people all over Boulder, Colorado in something that looks suspiciously like rickshaws. (The most charming one is the "Wedding Limo" in white with gold trim.) The carts attracted so much attention he got written up in all the local papers. Soon he got a call from Celestial Teas asking to advertise on the sides of his bike-driven carts and as it turns out, most of his revenue is from advertising!

Doug did his homework by traveling to a number of similar businesses around the country and asking their advice for his business plan. He got investors and everything! Now he is doing so well he has plans to branch out into other cities. He could be one of those people who has an IPO and gets on the Nasdaq, and then somebody else will have to write about him because, as I've stated, I'm sticking with small-time operators. But maybe we can still go to parties in his mansion!

Doug's company transports people for the most part—although I'm sure he also does small deliveries (no pianos, I assume)—but you can use this kind of bike business for many things besides transport. In fact, almost any business that can be done from a van or on the road, can be done with a bike and rickshaw (see "V" for Van-based businesses).

If you've got more imagination than money, get your hands on one rickshaw, make it really pretty, and spend your days driving it around where people can see you. I've already mentioned portable dog grooming in the last chapter, but you can do all kinds of things people need—and you can do them right now! If you're riding around on the city streets, people in cars are going to look at you. Get a name like "Help In A Hurry" and write a list of the kinds of things you do right under your name on the side of the rickshaw to give them the idea: Take down drapes and deliver them to the dry cleaners, and bring them back (and put them up again!) Pick up your kid from a party, or deliver food for a caterer. Just make sure your telephone number is very conspicuously painted on the side of your rickshaw so it's easy to see, and be sure you've got a cell phone with you.

If you don't like driving around in traffic, you can carry packages (and people) to their cars in a really large shopping mall with a really huge parking lot. You can help seniors or little kids or the disabled get around those big, unfriendly spaces, too. Who would pay you? Well, since you're just tooling around getting free advertising for yourself, no one has to pay you at all. However, if you really prefer this business over the "Help In a Hurry!" idea, the merchants in the mall might be interested. You just have to head into the main office and do a little selling. You're sure to be the first parking lot rickshaw person in your town. (And hopefully, the people you're transporting will love you and give you a tip.)

Can you think of any other loveable, attention-getting services that might attract advertisers without using rickshaws? Write them down. (Call friends and co-workers to help you come up with some more. That's good practice!)

C

Captain of your own ship

So many of us assume that dreams like this are for children, but just because a dream sounds grand or you've had it since you were a child doesn't mean it's silly or out of reach. If you have a dream of being a Captain, then that's what you must be. If you know how to sail a ship, here are some ideas. If you don't, do a search on the internet to find a school that will teach you. (Or better yet, find a captain who will take you on as an apprentice. That doesn't sound easy, but give it a try. You're sure to learn *something*, even if it's just that some captains won't talk to you!)

- Find someone with a yacht who needs it moved to a warm climate
- Be a ferryboat captain (I met one who had a degree in Philosophy!)
- Charter a boat for historical excursions on the rivers of the U.S.

Here's one of my favorite entries (in one of my favorite career books, *Cool Careers for Dummies* which you can find in almost any bookstore):

> "**Tugboat Operator**. This is a sailor's job that pays $50,000-60,000 and doesn't require long stints away from home. And the job market is good. Fear of oil spills has resulted in regulations requiring most large ships to be towed into dock by a tug. Most tug operators get their experience working on party boats or fishing boats, or by attending a two-year maritime program. See *International Organization of Master Mates and Pilots: www.bridgedeck.org*. See also: *jobxchange.com/xisetoc.htm* for job listings."

If being a captain is a dream you don't want to—or can't—presently turn into reality, don't abandon it. Do readings of books about sea captains or present a film festival of great sailing movies in a public place by the marina—or on someone's boat. (To earn some money from this endeavor, bring books and videos/DVDs to sell. Contact catalogs or shops that sell to sailors and offer discounts with tea and cake after the show.)

Cowboy

This is another dream that most of us just assume is impossible. Well, it isn't. The following comes from Joyanna, a Success Teams Leader in Toronto and Vancouver:

> Paul, an accountant, did not like his job. After unsuccessfully trying to find a profession he might like better, we discovered he really wanted to be a cowboy! Of course, Paul resisted, saying it was silly—how could you make a living that way? Paul's team didn't agree and brought magazines devoted to horses to the meetings. He committed to weekly homework of visiting local stables. Within a few weeks he signed up for a horse grooming course. Next, he took a course in horse massage! Now the team calls him the Horse Whisperer because of the special ability he has to connect on a profound level with horses.

The story doesn't end there. Paul got in touch with several ranches in Canada inquiring if they might be able to use his accounting skills...and got several offers! Paul jumped at one of them and will soon be doing accounting (and taking care of horses) at a ranch 100 miles from his home.

Film Critic

Being a critic doesn't automatically make you a bad guy! If you're wild about movies and you're seen as representing the viewpoint, for example, of twenty-something film audiences, you can be a film critic and write a column for local newspapers. Advertisers who want to reach the group of people you represent would be interested in the publication you're in and that means the publication would be interested in you. Make your viewpoint clear—write six sample columns about recent films you've seen and submit them to the local newspapers. Be sure to spell out just who you are and what group of people you speak for.

You can cut your teeth by starting out on the internet with your own newsletter and mailing your reviews to the filmmakers themselves, as well as everyone else you know. Let the local movie house know what you're doing. If you like a film that's showing there, the manager might direct people to your website.

The same goes if you want to be an art-, restaurant-, theater-, or music critic. Just make sure you're catering to a very specific audience and concentrate on building your readership. That will be your key to getting published (and paid!) (Remember, thinking is not a spectator sport. Keep taking notes.)

Coaching

What is a coach?

A coach helps people who feel stuck and need action. In that way, he or she is different from a therapist. The reason coaches can make such a huge difference is the same reason Success Teams and structured classes make a huge difference. Coaches, teams and teachers have new information people might not have themselves, so they can give needed advice. They often have personal contacts so they can help you get the right doors opened. They give you assignments and make you show up to account for your progress, so you actually take one step after another—whether you're a positive thinker or not. This is called "accountability" and it makes things happen like nothing else in the world.

Originally—after its use in sports, that is—"coach" meant career coach, and while the profession developed from a number of sources, I think the idea came mostly from big companies. When they'd fire a top-level executive, they'd pay serious money (over $15,000 per employee) to have a support person from an outplacement firm keep them company, guide them through the demoralizing process of finding a new job (or not), and so on. But corporations were by no means the only places to use coaching. I was one of the earliest people to be called a "career coach" in the U.S.—and I didn't work with corporations or their downsized ex-employees at all.

When these people became known as coaches, an entire industry opened up. Coaching basically means you meet on a regular basis with someone (you can coach via telephone or computer), and help them think of steps they can take to improve their situation. You're also there to encourage follow-through and accountability. If someone is supposed to make a phone call, you help them figure out who to call and what to say. And you check to make sure they did it.

How much do you charge? At this time, the corporate-downsized people are paying $300 to $900 a month for three sessions. But if the corporation isn't picking up the bill, that can be a little steep for an individual. You'll get a sense for the right fees by how many customers you get!

How to get started

Don't judge your effectiveness by how well your support works with your family. If you want to help them, find another life coach and send them to her. Families and friends have all kinds of resistance to getting advice from people close to them. But if you've found yourself trying to fix their lives since time immemorial, you've gotten great practice and you're obviously a good life coach. You can find out if it's right for you before you sign up for any coach training. Here's how:

First, find your niche (you'll see lots of options in the next pages).

Second, join any relevant organizations that have small discussion groups (like churches, National Organization for Women, etc.) Sit in on the discussion groups and help people. You'll get noticed. Explain that you're a coach. That kind of experience will show you who you are, and it will show other people as well. If you decide this is for you, there are two possible routes you can take to become a Generalist (a.k.a., Life) Coach:

1) get trained and certified by one of the new schools of coaching. You can figure on at least six months and about $4,000 dollars at some of them, less at others. (See *CoachU.com* and *Coachville.com*); or

2) just do it. Remember, if it's something you'd love to do, you have a talent and that will draw clients.

So, what can you coach? Start by thinking of how many people with different needs would benefit from having a coach. Here are a few that come to mind:

Food coach

My friend Gustav is a wonderful chef. His biggest complaint? "People don't know how to *eat*!" He decided to become a food coach.

"When people see how different tastes go together, they become gourmets. My job is to teach them how to really enjoy what they cook and serve." He is constantly coming up with imaginative new ways to create dishes that are out of this world. He is currently planning a website whose purpose is to build a mailing list and start selling his recipes. He's going to include a bulletin board and a free advice page. For more ideas, see "Cooking" below.

Budget coach

If you're good at keeping track of money, you should consider being a budget coach. You'd help people get out of debt, checking up on them every week or two and be someone they can call (like a sponsor in Alcoholics Anonymous) when they're having trouble sticking to their commitment but who gets paid. If you're someone who's really good at getting back on your feet financially, and if you've helped all your friends do it (probably free of charge), it means you've got something going for you and all you need is to be able to get near a phone three times a month for each client.

What else can you coach?

I just met a memoir coach—she'll help you write your memoirs by meeting with you on the telephone three times a month to hear what you've written and help guide you towards a successful book.

You can be a script coach or a book coach or a thesis coach. A writer I know used to send off drafts to his manuscript coach and loved getting it back full of notes and comments the next day.

I've heard good things about performance anxiety coaches—an actor friend of mine had become a director, not because that's really what he wanted but because he tended to freeze during performances at unpredictable times. He went to one of these coaches, and now he's acting without any problems and phasing himself out of directing.

Some people on my bulletin board have suggested that someone with social talents become a friendship coach which sounds like a sensational idea to me.

You should be looking at any/all of your strong points as possibilities (don't be modest!) Do you have a keen sense of style? Are you great at helping people put resumes together and prepare for job interviews? Is writing your strong suit? How about party planning? Or wedding planning? That's not a "planner," you understand. You'd meet with your client in person once or twice to set up their "to-do" list and you'd schedule phone appointments to keep them moving and help them troubleshoot problems. These are all areas where coaches are sought and paid (sometimes very well).

Home business coach

If you've started and run your own business, you can coach someone else to do the same. (Don't you wish you had had someone knowledgeable to keep track of you, help you get out there and start marketing yourself, remind you to keep up-to-date with your bookkeeping, tell you when you need an assistant, etc. when you were just beginning?)

Charisma coach

I kid you not. I knew someone who went to a class in How to Have Charisma. The teacher was so good that a number of students hired her to meet with them every two weeks to continue the training. She helped them look good, but only so they could forget entirely about how they looked! (They were allowed to look in the mirror only three times each day.) According to her philosophy, charisma came from having a strong center and looking at others rather than worrying about them looking at you. To build each student's center, she had them read philosophy and act in amateur plays! To teach them to look at others, she taught them to ask themselves what role any person they met could play in a movie. Because it was all too easy to fall back into old habits of self-consciousness or shyness, having a phone session with the coach twice a month was a very fine gift each student gave herself.

You know, of course, that there are singing coaches who get opera singers ready for a performance and there are riding coaches to train horseback riders. But did you know that there are organizing coaches who will set up your home or work space in person and then do follow-up meetings with you on the phone regularly to see how well you're doing at throwing things out, keeping your bills in one place and being careful about bringing new things into your home?

In a pinch, what could *you* show someone how to do? Without thinking about it too much, just move over to those nice, wide margins and start writing everything you can think of that you could teach to someone who just didn't know how to do it.

Cooking

If you love to cook, don't automatically sign up for Cordon Bleu or buy a restaurant. You might already know what you need to know to do what you love best, and you might not like owning a restaurant. There are lots of ways to earn money cooking that might suit you better.

Be a personal Chef

So many people don't know how to cook, don't have the time, or simply don't want to! If you were a personal chef, you could create and deliver the meals that busy working people (especially parents) and singles who just don't cook would want to eat. Maybe there's someone out there who likes custom meals, has special nutritional needs or allergies or has difficulty getting out to shop for food. Regardless, this is the perfect job for anyone who actually likes to make a meal.

What if you don't have a "legal" kitchen? Do what someone on my bulletin board did: rent the kitchen of a nearby church. It will surely be licensed and the church might be very happy to earn income at times they're not using the facilities themselves.

Word of mouth is going to be your most powerful advertising tool, so offer to cater local meetings (at cost, the first time only). Ask the store where you shop for the freshest foods to post a flyer promoting your service—and in exchange you'll promote their store. There are networking organizations (some of them charge a fee) that help personal chefs get hired: *personalchefsnetwork.com*, *pchefnet.com* and *hireachef.com*.

Run a private Dinner Club

This is an idea not many people think of, but those that have done it really love it (check the rule books in your part of the world but last I heard, a private eating club doesn't require the same licenses as a public restaurant). If you like to cook, try creating upscale dinner parties for singles. You need access to a nice, big house or apartment. See if someone will loan you his/hers in exchange for being at every party, or in exchange for getting publicity for his/her cooking/ catering. Invite someone with people skills to get the conversation rolling, or come up with a topic for discussion. I read about a couple who started that way, and were so successful they later opened up a restaurant. The end of the story is interesting: they found the restaurant required so much work that had nothing to do with their first loves—cooking and people—that they closed it and returned the action to their homes. The upshot was that they were much happier and made considerably more money as well.

Moral: All cooking doesn't have to take place in a restaurant. Think of some other places you might enjoy cooking for a profit. Here are some ideas to get you started:

1) Cook at flea markets or ethnic fairs. (No ethnic fairs in your region? Start one. Start a number of them in different locations.)

2) Cook special diets (like Atkins) and deliver them to people at work.

3) Cook on yachts and sailboats and see the world!

4) Be an itinerant cooking teacher and travel the country doing lunch-time programs for employees at corporations. Show them how to cook fast, simple, nourishing meals. Or do programs for students at colleges on

how to cook with a textbook in one hand, or how to cook economically without getting scurvy, or how to cook on a Bunsen Burner! (Go to an online used book dealer and see if you can find a grand book from my college days called *How To Cook A Wolf* by M.F.K. Fisher. The wolf in the title refers to the 'wolf at the door.' I still fondly remember a highly nutritious meal made from castoff vegetables discarded by supermarkets which was cunningly called 'Sludge.')

5) Do a professional video shoot of all your classes (many companies and colleges have the facilities for this and might be interested if it defrays some of your fee) and show them to your local public TV station (along with some kind of weird cookbook) to see if they want to do a show with you, or put the videos up on your own website and sell them (and the cookbooks) online.

D

Dive in the ocean

(See also "B" for Beach Bum)

Diving for a living is not the pie-in-the-sky type of goal it appears to be. There are many opportunities for certified divers, and more are being created all the time as sea exploration becomes a high-priority for governments and businesses. There's money to be made in scuba diving. Here are some ideas:

1) Move near the ocean and find any kind of temporary job to tide you over until the good stuff starts happening. Once there, start doing diving-connected activities for extra cash and to build lots of contacts. Scuba divers can make good money cleaning barnacles off the bottoms of boats at any salt water docks. All you need are sturdy brushes and a metal scraper. Make up cards and fliers and leave them in all the marina offices you can find. The work pays well and you can make your own hours.

2) Create a nestegg for your dream by saving your pennies so you can go on a diving trip. Your local dive shop will have all the information you need.

3) Contact reclamation projects for shipwrecks. Check out the military, police and rescue units and find out what they're looking for. Search for any employer who might pay for your training and/or move you out to the ocean.

4) Build more and more contact with friends who love diving like you do. Take classes and make friends with your dive instructor. You'll often find a door into something exciting (like underwater archaeology, which always needs volunteer divers).

5) Start a meetup group at *www.meetup.com*. The people who attend will know about all kinds of opportunities and ways to make money from diving.

6) Another way to get diving friends: put an ad in the Personal Column, "Wanted: Activity partner who loves scuba diving for enthusiastic talk and sharing information."

7) Craigslist (*www.craigslist.com*) has a section specifically for "activity partners". Even if you don't find them in your own town, you can find them in other towns, and start a friendship through emails and telephone calls.

8) Get in touch with divers through websites. Some can be found far from the sea, such as the Triangle Divers Scuba Diving Club in New England!

9) Find some discussions on Usenet Newsgroups for even more insider information and support. Here's what my search through Google groups found: One person wrote that he had just completed his Open-Water certification and dives in Alaska in November! He said he was going on a scuba trip but was hesitant as he had so little experience. An answer: "For your first dives, you can team with the divemaster as a dive buddy...Congrats on the O/W cert and your cahones to get in Alaskan waters."

10) Work in a dive shop. If you're not near the ocean, work on a dive website, at a diving school, at a diving equipment retail outlet.

Documentaries

As everyone will quickly tell you, it's expensive and difficult to make serious, feature-length documentaries and it's even harder to get them sold and shown. Oh, and everybody wants to do it, so the competition is fierce. It's almost impossible, ruinous, heartbreaking.

When the nay-sayers are finished, think about this: One, you don't need much money at all, depending on what you want to shoot. Two, you don't need experience or credentials unless you're looking for a job, so be your own boss. Three, no one wants to do the documentary you want to do anyway, so just search your heart and you'll find the subject that needs to be done. You'll see right away that you're the one to do it. Four, there are many places where you can show your documentary (depending on the subject). Five, Steven Spielberg started by making movies in his backyard as a kid. And Six, who can stop you?

You don't need to ask anyone's permission or get anyone's approval to make a documentary. You can make a high-quality short documentary on any subject you care about. Pick a subject that really matters to you and you'll find you have a special instinct for asking the right questions of the right people.

Start close to home. Do the story of your neighborhood: its character, how it came to be the way it is, its history; or the oldest people in your town, where they're from, what they've seen, how things have changed, what they want to tell younger people.

Or do a documentary about Love. Interview anyone who's willing to talk about what love means to them. If you want the real skinny, hide their faces and let them talk. You could do something fascinating here.

How about "Kids Today"? What do ten-year-olds care about these days in your neighborhood? How about comparing it with kids in other neighborhoods and see what comes of it? Or compare it with your parents' memories. Or your own.

The point? There are things that matter to you and nobody's filming them. Pick up your camera and shoot them until a story emerges. Then, go get the pieces you left out when you didn't yet know what the story would be.

Want some more ideas? Shoot a documentary on all the ethnic groups in your town: get interviews about their histories and donate them to your local library. They might put your documentary on their calendar of events and even ask you to address the audience afterwards. Or take your documentaries to the local movie theater. If it's a huge chain and won't let you, try the hall of some service club like the Lion's Club or the Veterans of Foreign Wars, and stage a documentary festival every few months. Advertise for people to bring in photos and stories that you can put into your film, and shoot some more!

Do a documentary about someone's family, and let them give it as a present at the next birthday of the oldest member. Interview the owners of any small business in town, from a dry cleaner to a diner, and put together a short film on the history of their store that they can show on a loop in their window (or at the local TV station). Volunteer to teach the craft of filmmaking to kids in school. See what happens when you put a camera in their hands and turn them loose. You might wind up with an Oscar and a stage full of kids to help you accept it!

Did that get your juices flowing? What's the subject of the documentary you should start making tomorrow?

Dairy farmer's relief pitcher

If you know something about dairy farming (or would like to learn) and sometimes wish you had your own dairy farm, but know perfectly well you'd never be willing to live and work there all the time, you can be a relief person for a dairy farmer. As you should know, a dairy farmer has to be there every day, morning till night, to take care of milking and caring for the herd. They never get a day off, much less a vacation in Florida for a few weeks in the winter.

You could step in like an angel from heaven. I don't know what kind of money arrangement you'd want to set up , but if you have the kind of work that's seasonal or that can be done from anywhere (internet-based for example), you might want to contact some of your local farmers to see if any of them need a vacation. Offer to help out for a day or two as an introduction for both of you. You'll know soon enough if you both have the tolerance for each other's ways.

Think about it, this could be a service, like a part-time employment agency. Find the sons and daughters of farmers who have moved to the cities because a full-time life of farming wasn't for them, but who also miss the beauty of the farms of their childhood. Maybe they'd like to be the relief pitchers. Why should it be all or nothing for them? Everyone deserves to have more than one kind of life if they want one. You can help them get it.

Day trip planner

Do you have a talent for thinking up fun ways to spend the day? Do friends ask you what they should do with visitors from out of town or bored kids on school holidays? You could start a service for people who would love day trips!

Have a free telephone message for great things to do with kids, romantics, seniors, creative types and adventurers each day. Post that phone number on supermarket bulletin boards or in the "Events" section of your newspaper. On some days you can add "I'll be taking up to 15 people on a tour of beautiful Wave Hill on Saturday at 11:00 am, rain or shine. Come if you love to read, stroll and take photos or if your kids have too much energy to be indoors. We've got an amazing historian coming along who turns historical sites into action movies when he talks. The cost is $10 per person if you bring your own lunch, $20 if you want a delicious basil chicken picnic with wine and dessert."

Next week offer a tour of the museums, galleries or even inside the studios of working artists in your town with an art historian: "The artists who have offered to open their studios will talk about their art and answer questions. Get on my email list for more instructions on joining me for a fantastic day! Come to *www.neatdaytripsforall.com*." (I made up that website, but you knew that, right?)

If you had a bicycle (or a motorcycle, depending on what your passengers will tolerate) with a sidecar (or that rickshaw again!) you could take elderly or disabled people for great trips through parks or any parts of town they might like to see.

If you need more ideas for what to do, you can use existing activities. Here's a pitch by an enthusiastic fan on my bulletin board for naturalist clubs.

Love Animals? Nature? Take a Day Trip to the Great Outdoors! Join a Naturalists Club. You will find all kinds of people who love everything outdoors...botany, geo-physics, birds, fish, tigers, lizards, you name it. And they are always networked to other Naturalists Clubs.

Naturalists Clubs always have walks and hikes and cross-country skiing and boating and camping activities of every kind. No matter your fitness level, there is something for you and your special interest. They often arrange work parties and preservation projects, too... (Ours were nesting boxes for Mountain Bluebirds; lakeshore clean-up for shore birds and shore fish and it was great fun. We met great people, too, with every interest, and found resources we never dreamed of. Age is no barrier.)

And here are some books to read aloud to your happy troupe during lunch:

"The Complete Walker" by Colin Fletcher. Colin has walked the Himalayas, the Grand Canyon, deserts, and the Rockies north to south, perhaps the Andes, too.

"Feasting on Wild Edibles" and any other book by Bradford Angier.

E

Escort

No, I'm not advising you to get into the steamy world of sex work. There are many other kinds of escorts. Any subject you're interested in has its visitors to your city. Some are celebrities and some are ordinary people who love what you love: photography, art collections, antique autos. Others just want to have a good experience in your town, and if you're one of those local treasures who know all the best places to eat, all the best shops or shows or music, you could make their visit a memorable one. If, for example, you know something about art history you can earn some money as an escort or tour service to corporations with visitors from out of town. Women travelers would probably be very happy to have someone to escort them to events like gallery openings.

There are also escort services on cruise ships where you can actually work as an independent contractor to be a woman's escort on the ship: you take her to dinner, dance with her, and entertain her with intelligent conversation. Nothing more than good company is required.

Author Escort

Publishers hire freelance escorts, too. An author escort, for example, is a sort of a personal assistant/minder to authors while they're on book tours, whose main job is getting them to the radio and TV shows, book signings and newspaper interviews on time. I've had wonderful escorts, hired by my publishers, and never would have found my way around without them. I found this article at *bluemooncommunications.com:*

> Author escorts are professionals who know the media of their city and can get you there on time. Often, they'll even book the media for you or at least provide you with a media list of people you can contact to secure interviews. All of this isn't cheap, of course, and rates usually range from $135 for an eight-hour day to $180. Some charge mileage or fees for booking media on top of that. But talk about a investment that is well worth the dollar! What good would it do you to schedule an interview with CBS This Morning or Oprah if you got lost on your way there and missed it entirely?

> The best way to find an author escort for nearly any city in the country is to contact the National Author Escort Network Pro Motion Network. Emily Liasy (pronounced Lie-zee) can find you just about anybody.

Expediter

I know someone who makes a really good living as an expediter. (I never heard of the job title before, either.) She works for insurance companies and contractors and basically stands in line to get their permits for them. She's got the personality for it, and doesn't become impatient waiting in line for six hours to get to the next level. Expediters get paid a lot of money because they push along (they *expedite*) the horrific and sometimes infuriating process of getting permits, and processing paperwork, which could otherwise hold up their clients' valuable business.

If you have unusual tolerance for the kinds of details that make others want to pull their hair out, you might be able to do something interesting with it. Call any company that might need your services and tell them what you do. (Import-Export people come to mind at once.) Write up a short sales piece that educates those who don't know what an "expediter" is to the glories of not having to worry about the problems you'll handle for them. Meanwhile, the rest of us will dream of being able to afford hiring you for ourselves!

There is no business that doesn't need an expediter, just some who haven't realized it yet. I've found expediters who help researchers find human tissues for research, and trucking businesses have expediter booths at their expos and shows.

But what I don't find (and would love to!) is someone who can expedite for individuals. Wouldn't it be great to have someone get through the details of purchasing a cell phone or digital camera or webcam or PDA for each person's unique needs? Who has the time to compare and understand these things? How about someone who can expedite your understanding of an insurance policy? Or an elder care facility for a family member? How can you trust the salesperson?

Of course, you can always scout out the details on Usenet newsgroups or do a deep search on the internet, but that's just not a good use of most people's time, and it might be worth some money to get someone to do that for you. Like, who can sleuth the truth about what a company is really like to work for? Who can understand the forms you have to fill out to get a grant or become a non-profit? The information is often available and people who don't mind fighting their way through books and networking and interviews and newsgroups might think it's no big deal...but oh, is it a big deal for the rest of us! If one existed, that's an expediter who just might get a lot of work.

How to charge? Like a lawyer with a retainer. You can charge $50 an hour or accept a retainer of, say $100 for up to 5...uh... expeditions. :-) If you set up shop, call me first. I need a lot of help.

Expert, become one

If you're someone who knows more than the average person about something (and everyone is), that makes you an expert. Don't assume you need higher degrees or formal training. Find what you already know and examine it carefully.

I had a client in the Bronx, years ago, a young mother who said the only thing she was good at was taking care of her kids. She knew she was a great mom and wished she could help other mothers, because she knew it was hard for many of them. But she had no confidence that anyone would listen to her. She had never finished high school and couldn't even volunteer at a community center because she didn't drive and had to wait for her husband to come home after work to take her.

I sent her (by taxi, at first) to an upscale NOW chapter full of wealthy, educated women who held discussion groups on different subjects one night a week. She sat in on one group saying nothing until one woman mentioned how hard it was to handle her infant child who was up all night. She jumped in with advice and her confidence had other mothers surrounding her the first night. Her advice worked and soon she became a group leader at the meetings. Before long, she was doing phone consultations any time of the day or night (she didn't mind a bit!) and the women insisted on paying her for her invaluable help. "You do more for my life than my therapist!" one said. "You do more than my obstetrician!" said another.

She later went back for her high school equivalency certificate and the women she helped taught her to drive. She fulfilled dreams she'd never attempted before because of the respect she got from the women she was helping. And she got that respect because she deserved it for her expertise.

Here's another example: I heard of someone who had worked as a secretary for an art restoration house for many years, and learned a lot more about antiques than most of us will ever know. She didn't consider herself an expert because the firm she worked for was filled with "real" experts. But she did know how many people watch the hit TV show Antique Road Show, and how much they wished they could find out what their antiques were worth, so she started her own one-woman antique road show. She'd travel to small rural towns to look for antiques for herself or for friends and would set up in advance (often in the local schoolhouse) an afternoon where she'd help people figure out what their antiques were worth. She carried many reference books with her and hooked up a computer as well, but working in the office of a restoration firm all those years, she saw first-hand how much people were willing to spend for what kinds of pieces, and her instincts were excellent. She helped people understand what their antiques were worth, and bought the ones she liked at what she could prove were fair prices.

A letter I received last year proves the point:

"Many people find old paintings in aunt Lucy's attic and have no clue as to what they actually have. An example: an alumnus from my college went to an estate sale and bought this huge painting for about $25. It is nearly 20ft tall, a portrait of three generations of men. He decided to donate it to the art department of the school if they would help him have its worth evaluated. His $25 purchase turned out to be an original Italian Master worth $20,000,000. Yes, that's twenty million. Dollars. The Italian government even brought a case against him to have it returned as a national treasure, but I believe it is still housed in the Fine Arts Department of Spring Hill College. You never know what treasures are out there, and how many people have no idea what they actually have."

If you become an expert in crafts fairs, for example, you'll add to your present knowledge by searching for lots of ways to bring in money that you didn't know about before. You might also have a website and a short newsletter (see "Mailing List") and use it to sell your items, or even better, to sell your expertise to other crafts people. This goes for absolutely any area that interests you, the more esoteric the better.

Don't know what area you want to learn about? Try this exercise: think of ten things you'd like to be an expert in if you could swallow a magic pill and have instant knowledge. Aerodynamics? Botany? Chess? Just let your imagination go. Write as many as you can think of in the margins of this page.

Now for the fun part. Just for a laugh, go to Yahoo.com or google.com and do a search for each word you wrote on that list. Go on, actually try it. Now take a look at what came up: those links—which are now just a click away—are all the information you need to start building your expertise right now! What if you find nothing for one of your items? No aardvark sculptors on the entire internet? It's unlikely, but it would be fantastic!! That means you got there first. The time has come for you to put up that website on your own.

Experts never want to stop learning, and these days it's easier than ever. You'll find books in your bookstore or online. You can go over to *www.soyouwanna.com* to find advice on how to do anything at all, from experts! You can find magazine articles on your subject in The Reader's Guide To Periodical Literature at your library. At one time, that huge set of books was my bible for learning about anything. Once you've read a number of articles on any one topic, you'll get a sense of what's going on that very few books can give you. And you'll get names and places so you can make contact if you want to learn more.

If you really want to be up to date in some field, to know what's going on today, head over to the internet newsgroups and read what the people in that area are saying to each other. Go to websites on your subject and get on their mailing lists, too. Pretty soon you'll be an expert in anybody's estimation. Here are some books that might help you with the process:

Become a recognized Authority in Your Field in 60 Days or Less
by Robert Bly, 2002

How to be an Instant Expert: 6 Steps to Being an Authority on Any Subject
by Stephen J. Spignesi, 2000

(If you need an expert yourself, take a look at *ExpertCentral.com*. They have volunteer experts to answer your questions.

F

Fix things

"I wish I knew how to repair antique dolls. Every time I need to get something fixed it costs more than the doll itself," said a neighbor with a small collection. I'm an avid book hunter, so it wasn't long before I found some out-of-print books on exactly how to repair dolls. My neighbor did some searching and she found that there's a woman not far away who actually teaches courses in doll repair! Since it typically costs $75 to fix a pair of "open-and-close" eyes on an old doll, taking that class might be a decent supplement to my neighbor's income. Where will she get the business, once she knows how to repair dolls? She can visit antique stores and offer her services, of course, but she can also do every bit of her marketing on the internet. She doesn't even need a website if she doesn't want to bother with one. All she needs is to do a search for "dolls" and "doll repair" discussion groups and bulletin boards on the internet. She can leave a comment on any subject and sign with her business name, such as "Bridget the Doll-Eye Repair Maven," or some such thing, with her email address right below. You don't have to be an expert to make a little cash fixing things. You just have to know where there's a need—and there's always a need somewhere.

If you like the idea but prefer a different niche, take a look at your own possessions and see which ones are most difficult to get repaired. Is it your piano? Or your lighting? Window screens? Can you imagine getting in there and making them work again? If you can, then there's a income source waiting for you. If you can't, find the people who can, and sell their services. You can be a sort of mini-contractor and pay them yourself, but for small items it might be more practical to take a percentage of their fee. You can run classes too! (Call a local church or community center and I bet they'll be interested. You'll be the master of ceremonies, and present a different specialist each time.)

Fix someone's life, starting with their apartment

You could call this the Get-A-Life Housekeeping Service. Supposing you cleaned people's apartments to earn your money. It's not a bad job, actually, but you might get bored. Now imagine that you worked for some overworked, single professional who had no time for a social life and was leaving too many empty beer cans in the trash. Wouldn't it be fun to fix his or her life? You wouldn't just clean their apartment, but also update their linens and decor and persuade them to invite interesting people home after work, where you will have created romantic dinners: your client needs only to light the candles and open the wine. You can also do this for couples. If they have very little time, they surely need their apartments kept in order, and they probably need some candlelit dinners, too.

The housekeeping part will keep you in cash and away from the desperation of finding clients. And your clients will come to trust you because they know you. It's a lovely idea.

Farrier

I live in New York City, and just assumed farriers (those are the people who shoe horses) all lived in Montana. In fact, there are many farriers in Westchester county, a city bus ride away. It appears that lots of people in Westchester own horses. To be a farrier, you either go to school and get licensed, or you become an apprentice and learn by doing (or both). Horses are precious animals so this is no job for an amateur. But if you love horses, this can be a very lucrative field. According to the American Farrier Association, there are 10,000,000 animals that require shoeing, and that number is growing all the time. Consider the fact that most horses need shoeing every 6-9 weeks, and you've got a big demand.

Check out the following websites: *www.farriers.com* has a worldwide directory for locating farriers. *Americanfarriers.org* is the official website of the AFA, and gives lots of information about becoming a farrier, costs and benefits, and meetings/events near you.

Flying, teach it

There's a whole world open to people who love all things aeronautical (I'm not one of them—my favorite part of flying is the nap), and it's not limited just to commercial pilots. A very nice woman came into my office one day and told me that her husband (an Air Force pilot) was retiring and that they'd soon be moving off the base: a big part of her life had always revolved around flying, and now she felt like she was losing that part of herself. What to do? Since her love was flying and she had a small plane pilot's license I suggested teaching; but she didn't feel adequate to teach in a classroom ("Oh, no. I have no aeronautics training," she said, as if I'd asked her to train fighter pilots!) I was curious, so to check out this meek lady's attachment to flying I asked a trick question: "Do you think I'm too old to learn how to fly?"

Her eyes flashed and she leaned forward with energy I hadn't seen until that moment: "No one is too old to fly!" she said.

"Look at you!" I said. "You're a natural preacher. You could teach anybody to fly." The passion was there, it was just hard for her to see herself that way. I don't know if she decided to take my advice, but if she had gone for it, the path would not have been complicated. Wherever her husband's work took them (probably a small town) there would be an airport close by and she could give lessons to novices; or she could start a flying club and bring the public in for demonstrations.

OTHER SUGGESTIONS: There's a wonderful site that almost changed my mind about being a pilot. It's called *pilotinterviews.com* and does just what it sounds like: interviews pilots. You can get a real taste of the pilot's life, and they also have a great resource list of training schools (looks like it's in Canada only, so check for similar sites where you are).

But a preacher can do more than teach a skill, a preacher can inspire. So I also suggested she get on the lecture circuit as a motivational speaker for corporate programs. Corporations are always looking for motivational speakers who are women, but they're conservative places, afraid of touchy-feely or New Age thinking, which they automatically associate with women speakers. A pilot, however, and the wife of an Air Force pilot—who had the fire in her that I saw when she said "No one is too old to fly!"—a woman like that would be welcomed into any corporation (especially one with a large population of female employees).

Fashion Designer

If you know anything about the field of designing women's or men's clothes, you also know it's next to impossible to begin without lots of money and lots of connections, and even then, it's a terribly risky, difficult business. You need a factory and a showroom and a huge staff at the very least. And many times, the stores that buy your clothes end up sending them back for a refund.

But years ago a friend took me to an apartment in New York where a designer's representative was running a week-long show with about 30 dresses and jackets hanging on one rack, and a stack of fabric samples on a nearby sofa. I chose a dress I liked. Each of the styles had samples in various different sizes. I found a size that fit me, and then chose two colors from the pile of fabrics on the couch. I did the same for a jacket. Then I wrote a check to the designer for two dresses and one jacket and I went home. Ten days later, my new clothes arrived in the mail.

This designer had representatives in at least 20 cities in the U.S. They were paid a percentage of what they sold, and they provided their apartments for showrooms. (Sounds like a nice job to me!) At her home, the designer called in her staff of stitchers to assemble only dresses that had already been ordered and paid for. And her faithful clientele waited eagerly to get notified every season with a letter containing hand-made drawings of her new designs and locations of her representatives. I thought the model was brilliant, and the clothes were perfect. (I wore one of her designs on the Oprah Winfrey show!)

This model for making and selling your own fashions is simply brilliant because it completely sidesteps all the barriers to becoming a successful designer. No advertising and no showrooms. You don't have to get in the windows of big department stores or sell them huge lots and find some way to survive for months until you're paid (while you live in fear that they'll come up with an excuse to return the whole lot to you and pay nothing!). Best of all, you don't have to go looking for financial backers, and you don't have to be part of the establishment. Until I learned about this I always cautioned people against trying to enter the fashion business. But now I eagerly explain how this designer worked, and I've seen a number of small, successful businesses come into existence as a result.

G

Gifts, make and sell them

There is big business in selling gifts—like Teddy Bears—to corporate employees, saving them the time and effort of going to stores before heading home.

But you don't need a warehouse full of Teddy Bears to do the same thing. Hang around flea markets and thrift stores and buy up loveable items with charm and create your own unique, one-of-a-kind gifts. I once saw half a dozen small dolls sitting on vintage handkerchiefs inside pretty teacups. Think of how many teacups don't have saucers (and how inexpensive they are!) and how many little dolls you can find who otherwise might never have a home. And how would you like someone to bring you a pretty little doll sitting in a teacup for a gift. You might want to make one-of-a-kind lamps from thrift store items like one I saw in a magazine recently—a lamp made from an antique Victorian high button shoe with a small pole coming out of the top and a pretty lampshade attached. It was beautiful and it sold for almost $400.

Gardening, how to earn money at it

I own a book published in 1894 called *An Island Garden*, by a woman named Celia Thaxter, who loved flower gardens and spent her summers creating them at her island home off the coast of New Hampshire. She got an early start on her garden during the snowy winters when she lived on the mainland, by planting seeds in empty eggshells where they would start sprouting in her greenhouse. In the spring, she'd head over to her island with many cartons of eggshells full of small sprouts for planting in her island garden.

For those of you who live in the tropics, this may seem an unfortunate necessity, but to this woman (and to me) it seemed like a delicious ritual. If you agree, there's no reason you can't replicate the whole mood. Wouldn't this be lovely? Everyone gathers at a friend's house during the cold days of winter and, under the guidance of an experienced gardener like you, they learn how to set up an indoor greenhouse.

You can represent the manufacturer of indoor greenhouses, if you like. (You'll find their ads in most home magazines.) Or you can show people how to create a good-enough greenhouse from inexpensive materials. Or you can create your own and sell it to them!

If that interests you, give a free talk on winter gardening at your local library (where you can have a signup sheet of people who want to know of your next presentation and build a mailing list). Be sure to get in the 'events calendar' of your local paper, and even run a classified or small space ad to offer this service. I'm sure there's a nursery—the one where you buy your own gardening supplies—that would benefit from offering your services at their location and would advertise your talk on their dime.

If you can wait for warmer weather, you can even take your group of students to visit her island. It's called Star Island and there are day tours during the summer from Portsmouth, NH. It's very tiny and very beautiful and you can still sit in a rocker on the veranda of the lovely white hotel that housed so many famous people of the time.

How to get hired as a gardener

1) Praise Yourself!

I heard of a young artist who loved flower gardens, but couldn't have one of her own since she lived in an apartment in the middle of Boston. She decided to tell everyone she met that she was a professional gardener and had a magical green thumb with dahlias (the dahlia part was true). Within months, she landed a full-time job gardening for a wealthy homeowner just outside the city and spent an entire year planting and maintaining a garden, which really did feel like her own. Anyone could proceed in the exact way she did: ask around and see if anyone might be interested. Figure out where the upscale people shop (or send their gardeners). If they have gardeners, and you're not a pro, you might want to sign on as an assistant until you are. It would help if you were associated with a local gardening association or a plant nursery. In the meantime, you can brush up on your gardening.

2) Offer A Specialty

One article I read featured a woman who designs, creates and maintains parterre vegetable gardens on Long Island for wealthy people. She is also an artist, and part of the service includes a lovely drawing of the garden-to-be. Quite a nice job, if you live near lots of well-off people and love gardening. There are many wonderful sites on the internet. These two looked good for starters: *www.mastergardeners.com* and *www.yourgarden.org.*

spinoff idea #1: Head over to the closest used book store and see if you can find old home and garden magazines or—even better—gardening books from long ago. You could make a specialty of selling them with your own website.

spinoff idea #2: I once saw an article, wish I could remember where, about a botanical illustrator who taught her craft to women in their homes. The photos were taken in a baronial mansion in England where they know their gardens. If you're an artist or you know one, you might think of doing something similar in your home town. If you hook up with any nearby botanical garden, you can find out what art classes presently exist, if any. Then, become a botanical illustrator and teacher by going to a class.

spinoff idea #3: If you become knowledgeable about the gardens of the world, or at least the gardens in a country you'd love to visit, you can put together a small tour. You can combine it with drawing and painting classes, or photography classes, or you can simply find really special places with a special angle, like heirloom flowers from seeds that have almost disappeared from modern gardens. You can make a literary gardening tour—the gardens of Little Women in Concord Mass, for instance. Dig up your favorite period novels and find every description of the gardens and see what you can make of it. (Maybe put on an evening's reading of garden excerpts from old novels.)

Gondolier

Yes, I said Gondolier. I saw a post on *craigslist.com* (a community website) offering a position for someone who wants to spend their days rowing around Lake Merritt in a gondola singing Italian songs for tourists. Sounds like fun for someone who loves singing and Italian culture!

In my search, I found an article about college grad, Chris Johnsten, a singing gondolier:

> Four days a week, the Great Falls native and graduate of Montana State University-Bozeman dons black pants, a striped shirt, straw hat, red scarf and red sash. Then he climbs into a gondola, acquires an Italian accent and spins tales about his mama and papa and how he landed a job in the middle of a desert. In between, of course, he serenades his riders with songs like "Santa Lucia," "O Sole Mio" and the best of Dean Martin.

If you're an actor or a singer or you just love to play make-believe, you can start searching for opportunities on the internet. The article's at *http://montana.edu/commserv/csnews/nwview.php*.

Geographer

I love geography. I always have. I love knowing soil types and how they determined the way humans lived; I love knowing what a big bump in the ground really is, and knowing the difference between a new river valley (it's shaped like a "V" and the water moves fast!) and an old river valley (it's shaped like a "U" and the water meanders around like a big snake.) I love history and there's no history without geography. I've also found, though some lovely listservs, that geographers are a passionate bunch. They all seem to love what they do.

I came up with this idea for geography lovers: be a freelance geographer who does research for novelists and historians and screenwriters. Wouldn't that be a great gig? The way to get started is almost certainly by word-of-mouth. Head over to a local college and sit in on some history classes. Post a flyer on their bulletin board saying that you'll help students with the geography part of their projects. Post an ad in a writer's magazine and an amateur history magazine. Or you can come help me with this novel I've been wanting to write for a long time that takes place in the Himalayas. Check out the website of the Association of American Geographers at *www.aag.org*, but don't limit yourself to American sites. If English is your only language, check out the Canadians, Australians and South Africans. And the English, God love them, who have done so much traveling for so long you'd almost think they didn't like being home.

Game, design one

You don't have to jump the hurdles of the game industry and get caught in the swamp of protecting your idea, or trying to bring in a prototype for 4 cents and wait two years for your royalties...that is, if they come at all. If you know that route and want to take it, great. But if you don't and you don't, try this: Invent a game that solves a problem—a Rejection game for salespeople, for instance. You can use a Monopoly-type board if you like, or put one on a screen for them to see, but essentially they'd be moving pieces or picking up cards that have little scripts on them for the typical rejections, designed to make people laugh and let off steam, get practiced, have answers ready by doing it fast and often, etc. Then you can create a brochure and sell your game—and yourself to run the workshop—to any organization that uses salespeople. (Salespeople put up with a lot of rejection and many companies pay for programs to keep them motivated.)

In the meantime, just go to a big bookstore and find the sales motivation section in the business section and see if you can think up a game—either a board game, or a game people can play face-to-face in the workshops you're going to run for them (for huge amounts of money!) when you become a guru!

While you're there, think of what other problem-solving games you could create: a game for teachers who have difficult students? dealing with toxic co-workers? getting through family gatherings?

H

House sitter (or "anything" sitter)

People want to be able to go away and know that their house, apartment, dog and plants will be in good working order when they get back. You'd take in the mail, open the windows, occupy the space to ward off intruders, and whatever else is needed to maintain the home until the owners got back. Word of mouth will get you most of your jobs, or you could advertise in your local paper or try and get work through an agency, like *housecareers.com*. You can also check out an online magazine with some good opportunities (and, from what I hear, some not so good.) It's at *www.caretakers.com*.

Home businesses

Great for people who'd like to see their kids now and then before they grow up and leave home—and a blessing for disabled people—working at home is also just something some of us love to do. (I've done it for the last 35 years and I'm not tired of it yet.) There was once a magazine, one of the very few I subscribed to, called Home Office Computing, and every feature was about another person who had a home business. I wish it was still around. I've found some online magazines, though, and so can you. Just do a search for 'home business' and you'll get some ideas. Unfortunately, they've got that bright and fiery edge that keeps them asking things like "Are You Thinking Wealthy?" and keeps making me feel all tired out. I really miss my homey magazine with its pictures of home offices and nice people with dogs on their laps.

In any case, there are endless ways you can earn money from your home. Some require that you go out to buy and sell and deliver services, while the main office is at home. Some don't require that you leave home at all; everything can be done by mail or phone or computer or messenger or employee (or carrier pigeon!), or by having your clients come to you. These are ideal for the homebound, and for people who just hate to dress up. Here are a few things you can do from home, on your own, without addressing envelopes or signing up for those shady offers that require investments. You can:

1) **Write** cookbooks or magazine articles about a subject you know. Or books like this one you're reading, which I'm writing from my bedroom computer at this moment.

2) **Instruct, coach or give advice** on any number of subjects you're familiar with, on the telephone, via email, or by having people come sit at your feet in your own living room.

3) **Take in children, plants, pets or other valuable entities** whose owners need them watched while they work or travel.

4) **Create things**—like an audiotape series from your telephone classes or nifty lures for fly fishermen or Halloween costumes—and sell them on the internet.

5) **Start a cottage industry** like weaving or hand-painting on cloth for dinner napkins, tablecloths, bedroom linens for bigger companies.

6) **Do graphics** or editing or proofreading or translating for publishers or authors or anybody who needs it from all over the world.

7) **Make desserts** for local restaurants who are often very happy to offer locally made fresh and delicious desserts to their customers. Take some samples of your cheesecake or brownies to eating places near you (don't forget old-fashioned diners) and let the boss try them out. Holiday desserts can be sold at gift stores, flea markets or your own table or roadside stand.

8) **Make meals** for working people on special diets. When it comes to special diets like The Zone, Dr. Atkins, vegetarian, etc., I'm always surprised at how few restaurants serve them. What if you put up flyers in strategic places offering to deliver special lunches and/or dinners to people at work? You'll have your own list of clients (hopefully in the same building so you won't be traveling all over town every day). They can call in their orders by 3:00 pm the day before (to your home answering machine) including their credit card and expiration date and you'd always get paid in advance and wouldn't have much paperwork to worry about. If your kitchen at home doesn't pass health inspections (they can be pretty stiff), rent one by the hour. I know someone who did just that: "I rented a church kitchen near me which served meals for the elderly and therefore was certified. They only needed it at noontime and were glad to get the extra money I provided." (She also had to get a "food handler's" permit of the kind every food worker gets. Inquire at a church kitchen near you.)

9) **Be a freelance techie**—If you have Information Technology skills but don't want to be a full-time employee, try this site: *www.elance.com* for freelance work. It's been called "a sort of eBay for freelance projects." All the neat stuff you can do is shown right on the sites below. Incidentally, they're great models for web businesses you can do. They use every kind of technology you might want to develop (from telephone classes, email classes, instant messaging, teleseminars, etc.), and you can sign up on Paypal or other internet payment options. Study these sites well. Look at them as if you were an owner, not a viewer, and see if they interest you: *www.youcanworkfromanywhere.com.*

10) **Work with a school to teach online.** One woman, who had health problems and was virtually homebound, didn't know what she could possibly do from home. I found out she loved classics—I always look for a passion as my starting point—and here's what we came up with: She could teach classics online, to kids in public or private school classrooms, with links, exams, paper writing: she's the teacher—maybe the only online teacher in the school—and she's also a tutor, who can charge by the hour or a flat rate for the semester. She's got the credentials, and this way a school could tap in without nearly as much money or commitment. She could offer her class to a number of schools. She could look up all the relevant websites and discuss them on her own website. Maybe get kids to create their own classics website, from the point of view of their character: The World According to Sisyphus, etc. Why not teach a bit of ancient Greek and have sound available too? All the resources and technology are out there, accessible from the comfort of home.

11) **Start a babysitting agency.** A woman with similar health problems ran a babysitting business from her home. She matched up babysitting jobs (for professional couples) with babysitters (adults, not teenagers). She would get a cut of the babysitting fee, like a temp service. Business grew by word of mouth.

12) **Be a transcriber for health agencies.** Check with the hospitals and the doctor's offices in your area. Even though they may have a full-time transcriber, they often have a need for someone to fill in when there's over-flow typing to be done. Winter is the busiest time for doctors, so you may be hitting them at just the right time if you start looking now. Learning medical terminology is not too hard to do; I took the course many years ago and it was only offered on an independent study basis. I'd bet you could borrow a recent book from someone who just got through with theirs to get yourself up to speed. Depending on where you live, arrangements could be made for you to pick up or drop off the work once or twice a week (perhaps even less if they don't need the finished product right away), and someone may even be able to pick it up or drop it off to you.

13) **Telecommute.** If you want to work from home but aren't ready to break loose and be on your own, telecommuting may be the answer. You can find a number of sites on the internet offering jobs that allow you to work from home via computer. A quick search brought up the following: *www.sunoasis.com*, which offers editing and copywriting jobs, and The International Telework Association and Council (*www.telecommute.org*) and JFP-Telecommute Programming Jobs

(*www.jfpresources.com/jobtele1.html*). There you'll find up to date telecommute job ads for programmers and web developers. Make telecommute-friendly employers aware of your existence by posting your resume.

As with everything, you have to be careful about what you sign up and pay for. Check out *www.WAHM.com*. It's a good resource to help protect you from scammers. Cheryl Demas runs the site (she's published a couple of books on working from home) and she also has a page for job sites and listservs to help you in your searches.

I

Information broker

If you're someone who spends too much time surfing the internet because you love to learn about everything and you wish you could share the amazing information you find, you can be an information broker—which is a fancy name for someone who researches things for people who don't have the time to do it themselves. If you want to get into a competitive, high-paying field and you don't mind words like "demographics," "patents" or "focus groups," you might be able to work for some deep-pocketed companies. Look at these words from a company pitching their information broker training service:

"You will be in a position to save companies many thousands of dollars because their information gathering is inadequate or nonexistent. For example you'll be able to report things like:

-A prospective employee has already filed for workman's compensation on their last three jobs.

-An applicant has a criminal record or negligent driving record.

-A new client has past due accounts and bad debts at many other businesses.

-A client or vendor already has lawsuits pending, and the court has already awarded a $250,000 judgment against them."

It sounds like they know what they're talking about because they've hit on the two best ways to get a company to hire you: 1) demonstrate how you will make them lots of money, 2) demonstrate how you will protect them from losing lots of money.

But if that kind of work makes you feel like never surfing the net again, or you just don't want to spend ten-hour days in front of the computer (or never want to have a corporate boss), you might like a less competitive and far more interesting way to use of your love of finding information—and that would be to help micro-businesses and self-employed people. Imagine if a single mother of two with a day job, who has decided to breed and sell trained ferrets, could email you to do a search for all the places that breed or train ferrets—information about how to keep them healthy, who buys them, what kinds of licenses she'll need, and where ferrets have been mentioned in magazine articles in the last few years—and spend $25 to $100 to have that information waiting for her when she's through putting the kids to bed at 9 p.m. She might actually have a chance at a successful income stream and be very happy to pay you for your time.

I'm convinced that if micro-businesses had a freelance cyber researcher like you and a part time administrative assistant helping them, we'd see a lot more of them surviving and flourishing than we do now. And, pardon my soapbox, but I think successful home-businesses and one-person businesses are essential to the survival of our neighborhoods and the people in them. After all, chain stores and corporations pull money out of the community while tiny, local businesses spend their money right there. Okay, off the soapbox.

Why not specialize in working for freelance writers?

You could offer your service to freelance writers, too. They always have to do a lot of research to prepare magazine articles, and could write many more if you'd do all that research for them.

spinoff idea: build a mailing list of writers.

If you're feeling ambitious, you might try building a mailing list of freelance writers who wait to hear from you with suggestions about the new Latest Thing they could write an article on. You might want your information to be delivered via a paid subscription to a newsletter. Most newsletters have trouble getting paid subscribers, but if your newsletter will clearly help writers increase their income, they'll pay for this one.

Even easier, you can have a paid-for service with no newsletter, just an email, like "Hi Everybody. If you're scouting around for a topic for your next article, you might want to take a look at the new place ferrets have begun to occupy as replacements for watchdogs in homes and factories. There's a bunch of information and I've found three experts you can interview on the subject, to boot."

I've heard of a load of books about being an information broker. I don't know if any of them are useful because I don't have them in my hands. See if you can look through the ones that are in print at your local bookstore to establish if they're actually useful to you (and/or go to the internet and look up the authors to see what they're up to these days. That way, you'll be your own information broker, right now):

Building & Running a Successful Research Business: A Guide for the Independent Information Professional by Mary Ellen Bates

Super Searchers Make It On Their Own: Top Independent Information Professionals Share Their Secrets for Starting and Running a Research Business (Super Searchers Series) by Suzanne Sabroski

Super Searchers Go to the Source by Risa Sacks

Super Searchers on Competitive Intelligence by Margaret Metcalf Carr

Super Searchers Do Business by Mary Ellen Bates, Reva Basch

Find It Online: The Complete Guide to Online Research by Alan M. Schlein

Information Brokering: A How-To-Do-It Manual (How-To-Do-It Manuals for Libraries, No 86) by Chris Dobson

The Information Broker's Handbook by Sue Rugge

Researching Online for Dummies (with CD-ROM) by Reva Basch, Mary Ellen Bates

The Invisible Web by Chris Sherman, Gary Price

If you were an information broker, who would you love to have as clients? Think of what you'd enjoy learning. That will point to your answer.

Inventor

I have met a lot of brilliant people who had great ideas for inventions that never saw the light of day because either 1) they didn't know where to start (patents? prototypes? licensing? Who do you talk to if you want to sell something? How do you tell someone about your invention without having it stolen?); 2) they lost faith that their inventions would sell to a mass market (how to produce it cheaply enough/get a fair royalty from people who buy it); or 3) they got so caught up in the legal and financial complexities of trademarks and registrations that they had no time or energy left over. That's a real shame, because the world could have used their creations.

If you have a knack for problem-solving and an ability to envision what it would take to do certain tasks easier or better, then there might be an inventor inside of you waiting to come out. Keep in mind, your inventions don't have to be limited to gadgets like an improved can opener; you can invent new organizing systems or software for children or a new technique for shooting video. And I'd like to ask you to forget all about trademarks for now and just think about which of your brain children you'd love most to see become real. You should also know that there are more ways to bring your inventions to the world than through mass marketing.

Example: I invented Success Teams in 1975 to help people solve the problem of getting what they really wanted without all the fancy connections that big shots have. I didn't try to get Success Teams patented or to sell them to a marketing company, because I knew that my ideas would be successful when people saw for themselves how effective they were (plus, I knew that anyone can rip off just about anything in name: the key is to make the substance yours alone). How did I do that? By getting the word out any way I could. I ran workshops, I went on the radio, and I wrote my first book, *Wishcraft*, so by the time people all over the country started hearing about Success Teams, they had also heard my name...

There are other ways to attach your name to your invention, such as becoming an expert (see "E" for Expert) and publishing articles in the right places. (You'd know what your right places are better than I would. If you don't, that's your first research project! Find the publications that deal with your kind of invention as soon as you can.) If you find it difficult to get published by the establishment, write and self-publish your own books or eBooks, set up your own e-zine and start writing articles online. Send the address via email to all the people and places you want to know about it, so lots of people hear your name. Can you get ripped off? It's possible , but if you're well-known as an expert it's not an easy thing to do. So be sure to become well-known! Below, I've listed some resources for inventors—they're a huge presence on the web, and offer tons of information to their fellow creators. I've also included an excerpt from my bulletin board with advice about trademarks from people who have tried to bring their inventions to market.

www.inventorsdigest.com has been around since 1985 and claims to be "America's *only* inventors magazine." You have to subscribe, but it's full of articles, information and help for inventors in every category, and is probably a good starting point to see which direction you want your invention to take.

The United Inventors Association (*www.uiausa.com*) is "a tax exempt, not-for-profit corporation formed in 1990 solely for educational purposes. The mission of the UIA is to provide leadership, support, and services to inventor support groups and independent inventors." A quick glance at this site shows a lot of information, resources and connections to the community of inventors with an emphasis on protecting your invention. I was relieved to find what appears to be a very legitimate site, because I often feel wary of the offers made on TV for inventors. Call me paranoid but if I had something I thought was really innovative, I wouldn't want to share it with people who advertised right next to infomercials.

And here are some sites recommended by the goodhearted geniuses on my bulletin board:

United States Patent and Trademark Office: *www.uspto.gov/main/trademarks.htm*

Trademark: Legal Care for Your Business & Product Name (Nolo book)

www.loc.gov/copyright

J

Job Search Club

Start one. I started a few of them once (and read about a priest in Pittsburgh who did the same). Mine worked like a Success Team. Everyone met once a week, went over the classifieds together and prepared each other for interviews (we even kept each other company on the big day). There are lots of ways to make the unbearable process of getting a new job much easier (even fun!) You can use a video camera for mock interviews until everyone has their skills down pat. You can help each other with resumes—which always need re-tailoring for every interview—and even mail them out together. These are such loaded activities that trying to do them in isolation can cause paralysis.

This is the best way to conduct a job search and avoid isolation, but it can also be a good source of income. You can be a facilitator for these clubs and charge a small fee (say, $15 per person for each meeting) or conduct them via phone and computer if you want to cover greater distances and have fewer people competing for local jobs; you could do all the mailings, help people write their own "Situation Wanted" ads, and search the net for job sites and interesting opportunities. That would move you into the area of employment agent, which can be very profitable.

Think of some variations on this idea. What group besides job-searchers really needs a support group to help them get into action? What small activity club would you love to be a part of? Don't forget to check your ideas for H-Levels!

Journal Keeper

There are so many people who would love to keep a journal, either of what they're doing with their business, or just their thoughts in general, or what their lives have been about. Luckily for them, the weblog, or "blog," has arrived (see "W" for Weblog). No, it's not a monster movie, but an ingenious and simple way for people to keep a record of anything important in their lives and share it with the world via the internet. But most of those people don't have the time or the technical confidence (it's really easy to do) to create and update a blog. If you learned the very basics of blogs and consulted with clients to gather their information (photos, writings, etc.), you could create a nice little business.

For instance, say you know people who are homebound and just can't manage to write their journal, but want to have a record of what they're doing and/or thinking. They would call you (or you could visit them) and give you whatever they'd like to include in their journal; you would then put together a weblog with vignettes and photos from their lives and maintain it for them. You could create even more interest by teaching a course on making journals—including writing, photography and a little technology and bring in new clients. It's very hard to write about your own life, and it would be a wonderful thing to help people this way: they dictate, you write; then you put up the blog, enter the photos, help them assemble an email list (even if you have to call their long-lost relatives in Cincinnati to do it), and you make the whole thing work!

Junk rehabilitation

It's not news anymore that shabby is "in" and a lovely book called *Shabby Chic* even gave it a name a few years ago. If you can see the beauty in an old wooden chair or chest of drawers put out on the street or found at the thrift store, then you could put your love of their hidden beauty to work stripping and restoring pieces, and selling them (if you can bear it). Even if you don't know a thing about restoring furniture, pretty much anyone can strip a chair or an old table. All you have to do is invest in some paint stripper or remover, some scraping implements and steel wool. Apply the paint remover and strip away! If you want to learn more (which you probably should) check out *The Furniture*

Doctor by George Grotz and *Furniture Repair and Refinishing* by Brian D. Hingley and Timothy O. Bakke.

Advertise or bring your own pieces to show at flea markets, antique shows, and used furniture stores or have some fun and get a colorful truck to drive up and down the city streets with a loudspeaker hawking your wares! (For more on this, see the spinoff idea for Knife sharpener and kettle repair under "K".)

Jogging Buddy

If you love running—and can keep a cheerful conversation going while you do it—you could be a jogging buddy for people (individually or in small groups) who want to get in shape but lack the discipline to haul their tired carcasses outdoors on cold mornings. If you know how to gently motivate people and can teach them good running form, you'd be performing a valuable service. You could run your service like a club with membership fees, or charge per outing. You could cater to special groups like seniors or new mothers, and put out a newsletter with success stories and events to generate interest. You could sell prepared meals for them to take on their way, to help them eat the way they should. Once again, the internet will be your best friend. Start a website, get your mailing list together and put some flyers up where people shop or wait to have their cars fixed.

K

Knife sharpener and kettle repair

Think how many of these quaint occupations have been forgotten as we've become more modern and efficient (and wasteful). But now there's a whole revival going on in hand work, and people are paying more for the personal touch. A few years ago I heard a loudspeaker below my window calling out, "Knives and scissors sharpened, kettles repaired!" I looked out the window and saw a wonderful thing: a renovated old truck with an open back, colorfully painted with gaudy lettering. It was so appealing, I gathered all my knives and scissors and ran downstairs to line up with many of my neighbors. It was a lot of fun—a real neighborhood scene—and besides, who remembers to get their knives and scissors sharpened? This was a real, direct service business. Since then, I've dreamed about driving one of those charming trucks around different neighborhoods, calling out something for sale on the loudspeaker. If the idea appeals to you as well, think of some other services you might offer: Shoe repair? Photo portraits? A traveling magic show that sells magic tricks? Peaches, pears, watermelons? (My mother tells me people went down the streets of Detroit in 1915 calling out "Water Melones! Water Melones!" It strikes me as a fine tradition and one that should be maintained.)

spinoff idea: Those colorful, open-sided trucks would be great for selling many things, but where can one find such a truck? Well, if you're a mechanic/blowtorch artist/junkyard lover, how about rehabilitating and decorating old trucks and setting up a website where we could find you and order a couple?

Knitting clinic on a weblog

Now here's an interesting thought that might be new to you. (See "W" for Weblog first, if you have no idea what I'm talking about.) You can now show short video clips on a weblog, and that makes it possible to teach handcrafts like knitting on the internet from your home! How about a "knitting clinic" where people who have problems with some aspect of their knitting come online and get help from you? If you had some traffic coming through to your site you could make your income from advertisers.

If you have a specialty in knitting (or any other craft) you can go on a search engine and find the discussion groups on your subject, or go to relevant websites and their bulletin boards. The way to "advertise" is to leave a very helpful message with some great tip or technique and have your name and blog address in the signature, such as: "Gert Jones, *knittingandtattingclinicblog.com*" or suchlike. (Sorry, I get a bit nutty when I'm inventing imaginary names for little businesses. I'm sure you can do better.)

What else can you teach this way? Soon it will be possible to have much longer videos and more efficient webcams, so don't limit yourself with present technological limitations. I have a hunch medical schools are already teaching open-heart surgery with a version of this technology, but what can *you* teach? Kite building? Small engine repair? Success with African Violets? Making a white sauce without lumps? I know there are some instructional shows on television, and others that can be ordered from specialty video stores, but this would be instant gratification. A weblog would be waiting for those who want it, on the internet, any old time.

Karate philosopher

This may sound like a wacky idea at first, but bear with me for a moment. If you love the martial arts, you know how rich the philosophy behind them is. Other martial arts lovers feel the same way. There's a market for booklets, websites, even full-length books which would be popular as gifts to karate students by their friends, parents or teachers. Gather together an anthology or the most important quotes from books in the public domain (ancient books are the best, anyway), unless you already are a karate philosopher, in which case you'll have a long term commitment on your hands of actually creating, writing and publishing a book. I was thinking of something shorter and easier to produce.

You might get the maker of karate equipment and outfits to sponsor your book if you put their ads in the very last page of the book. With such arrangements, the sponsor often finances you by buying a few thousand copies up front, before they're published. I've heard of such arrangements before.

(Hint: If you're not a martial arts lover, replace the word "karate" with something you love more, and then see if you can apply the idea to your own personal passion.)

Keelboat recreational river vehicle

A keelboat is a covered river boat with a keel and shallow draft but no sail, propelled by rowing, poling, or towing, and used for transporting freight. Small ones would be wonderful for Sunday picnics on a small river in a city park. If you know how to build boats—or you know someone who does—do some research to find out what the legalities are locally (Can you just put a boat in your hometown river? Does the city want a license? Or a different kind of boat? What about the rules in nearby towns? Or a stretch of river on a farmer's land. You can always suggest he or she create a campground or a picnic ground—maybe even add a couple of buffalo and an electric hookup for trailers or RVs? Wait, wait, I'm getting out of control here. But you know how I feel about helping farmers get extra income. If you don't, see "D" for Dairy farmer's relief pitcher).

It may be possible to build these small, shallow boats with canopies to keep the sun off, and a small bench around the inside so people can sit, trail their fingers in the water and have a small picnic on a low table you could build in the middle of the flat bottom. I was on one of these in Thailand and they're quite wonderful.

Using keel-boats this way would be a novelty, which means if they catch on and you create your own small "Armada", you can bring in revenue from advertising on the sides or canvas tops.

You can get started by building a single boat to see if there is a market in your town. But don't stop there. Check out other small towns, too. Maybe you'll get some commissions to build more. If you're set up to do that, you're in the boat-building business and your clients could be the park departments of different towns.

If this idea appeals to you but you couldn't build a boat if your life depended on it, just find a boat builder who can. If you don't want to pay a prohibitive price and you'd like to work with somebody who needs the money, word-of-mouth in a not-too-fashionable fishing village might find you a real master. You might also get a seat in heaven if you kick start some kind of small economic boom in that business, that village, or that boat-maker's life.

Kids

If you love being around children—and not all people do—it means you have a talent for it. Just add your other talents to the idea of working with kids and you're sure to come up with something interesting and new. You don't have to go through the public school system. Instead, you can offer Outdoor Saturday Afternoon Rock and Roll Camp with a performance for parents and kids that evening at a family fee of, say $45. Or "mountain climbing" on a local hill while you tell mountaineer stories and top it off with a mountain climbing movie shown outdoors at a picnic ground.

One way or another, you need to be using your talent with kids, and they need someone like you, too. The best part about working with kids is that it can be part of so many other ideas: like writing (a two-day writing camp) and photography (ditto). I like the idea of capping off with an evening's performance of some kind. In this case, a reading or a photo exhibit of the work done by the class that weekend. I think you'd be sought for repeat visits.

Here are some more possibilities:

Kites and kids, traveling exhibit and workshop!

Follow the fairs and flea markets and bring materials for making kites. Bring some great ones to sell, and some greater ones if you want to have an exhibit. If you've really found some exciting historical material about kites, you might have a performance in you, one that can be done at county fairs or school assemblies. Most important, hold a contest after a kite-making class. Finance yourself by selling kite supplies and videos (if there are any—and I bet there are).

If kites don't do it for you, ask yourself this question: Is there anything else you could use this form for besides kites? Give it some thought until you find something you enjoy and, in your mind, replace "kites" with what you like better.

Kid's Farm visits

Find a nice family farm and arrange a program that brings city kids on a day trip to the country to experience life on a farm. For those of you who love the idea of getting away from the city and living a more natural life—say, raising horses or running an apple orchard—you'd be loved by kids and farmers alike (and earn some income to boot) if you could help farmers bring in some income this way. Here are some more ideas:

- "Farm stay" for vacationers or foreign students' semester abroad programs
- Visiting programs by naturalists or other teachers
- A class in Farm Economics: How to run a farm for a profit
- Summer stock theater
- Traditional American cooking school
- Computer support center
- Assisted living home
- Land rental for animal refuge (See also "A" for Animal refuge).

130

L

Living history specialist

If you've ever had the feeling you were born in the wrong century, you should check into this wonderful world. ALHFAM (The Association for Living History, Farm and Agricultural Museums) calls itself "An Organization of People who bring History to Life," and lists openings in living history museums around the country. Here's a small sample:

> The 1812 Homestead Educational Foundation is a working farm of the 1830's dedicated to the preservation of early American Heritage. Director must have knowledge of pioneer life with skills in colonial cooking or spinning or weaving or animal care or gardening or shingle making or lessons in one room school house. Duties include: scheduling school groups, promotion, staff training, development of new programs, grant writing, grounds-keeping, visiting schools, and attending workshops. Salary: $1400 - $1800 per month plus housing and meals. Medical insurance available. Willsboro, N.Y. e-mail: pokomac@aol.com.

This might be fun for would-be actors:

Living Historical Interpreter-Female Role
Location: Recreation Area in Western Kentucky and Tennessee Salary/Benefits: $21,320, $125/month health insurance allowance, 10 paid holidays, 15 days paid leave. Starting Date/Duration: April 16, 2003/Permanent position. Qualifications: 4-year college degree and some related experience. Duties: This full-time position serves as a living history interpreter on an active mid-19th century farm with 16 restored log structures. The position plans and demonstrates 19th century domestic work including wood stove and hearth cooking, spinning, weaving, domestic

trades, gardening, and special events for the general public and organized groups. The successful candidate must be available for weekend and holiday work, have a warm and enthusiastic demeanor, be team-oriented, and quality customer service driven. USDA Forest Service. Find out more by visiting *www.lbl.org*.

Have you ever dreamt of running a farm? In another century?

Historic Farm Leader, Golden Pond, KY
Duties: This full-time position oversees the daily operations of an active mid-19th century farm with 16 restored log structures.
(jtaylor@LBLAssoc.org)

If you're interested in working with kids and having a lot of fun, check this next one out; the best part is that it's seasonal work, leaving the rest of the year open for your other goals. (Of course, if your goal is to write historical novels, you can do it in the evenings, right on the farm.)

Seasonal Program Interpreters, Herndon, VA
Learn to teach early to mid 20th Century rural & agricultural history. Lead programs for school and scout groups. Learn to drive a tractor and give hayrides. Work with farm animals including cows, sheep, goats and more. Work in the Frying Pan Country Store. Learn about gardening, crops and farm equipment. Enjoy being outdoors. Full or part-time position available.

Love consultant

Single professionals are often so busy they have no time to fall in love. They have no time to find dates, no time to learn how to entertain them and no time to create a pleasant, romantic environment in their homes to invite them to. A love consultant's goal would be to fix all those areas. If that's something you know how to do, you can provide this needed service.

132

For example, you could help someone develop his or her romantic side by assigning books to read and old movies to watch just before falling asleep. You could advise them about the people they're meeting at work, help them figure out who seems worth getting to know better and how to talk to them. Then you could help them set up their homes with the right decor, music, lighting, even ice-breakers like fun board games to fall back on when the action flags.

See yourself as a director preparing someone for the romantic lead of their lives. You might be brilliant at it. Every success will bring you more referrals.

Start a Learning Center

If there is no adult learning organization in your town, start one. It's not hard. Just find specialists who are really good teachers, rent different locations for the classes and advertise in the local paper. Here's how I'd start:

FIRST STAGE: At a local church that has lots of non-religious programs for the community, arrange to use their space a few nights per month to start with. Take one night for yourself, if you like. Pick a topic (from memory, here's what I've seen in catalogues of adult learning centers: installing solar panels, how to make movies, computer skills, start a mail order business, salsa dancing, etc.) Design a 1½ hour presentation. Here are some guidelines:

1) Ask everyone why they came and what they're hoping for unless you have too many people, in which case you can say, "Does anyone want to answer?" and wait for people to raise their hands

2) Give a synopsis of what you're going to talk about

3) Present a problem that people typically run into and why they're solving it the wrong way

4) Show them the best way to fix it/do it, etc.

5) Ask for questions

6) Offer materials for sale, such as books or tapes you've found valuable, or your own books and tapes, if you have them

7) Ask for their email addresses so you can notify them of other events

8) Hand out evaluation sheets and ask what kinds of classes they'd like to attend in the future.

Get someone you know who is willing to give a different presentation. Everyone too shy? Find a schoolteacher or a lawyer or a singer. They like to stand in front of audiences and entertain them and they're usually pretty good at it.

SECOND STAGE: Contact local authors or teachers and other interesting people and ask them to present. Build and build. Presto, you've got a Learning Center. You'll never need a location, just rent inexpensive places to hold the classes and don't tell anyone where they'll be until the registration fee has been paid.

M

Money

The biggest obstacle to dreams I hear about is lack of money. There are several reasons why we assume our dreams need vast sums of money. Some of them are based on what we hear ("You need a fortune to start a theater/ranch/catering business, etc.") and others are the tricks our resistance uses to keep our dreams at a safe distance. But money isn't the obstacle you think it is—most of the ideas in this book require little or no start-up capital. If you look around, you'll find that the best ventures start with creativity and a real love for the idea. That's why I ask you to drop your assumptions about how much money things cost, and instead check your levels of happiness with every idea here. If you can find something you'd love to do, there's always a way to do it without much money.

So, if you think money is your big obstacle, ask yourself two questions:

1)   If you didn't need a lot of money to start, what would you love to do?

2)   How many ways could you do that without money?

If you need some input, start planning an Idea Party right now. Go to my bulletin board and/or bring as many helpful people together as you can and say, "I want to do X, but I don't have the money to start. Any ideas?"

Money, how to live in paradise without it (in a mansion, yet!)

Of course, you need a minimum amount of money to live anywhere. But to live in a place that feels to you (and lots of rich people) like Paradise, it takes serious money. Or does it? There is work in every resort, and not just domestic or hotel or restaurant work. Just don't think "job," think "needed services you can do for money."

I learned this from a woman I met who decided she simply had to live on a special and very fashionable island in the Caribbean, so she took a job in the local ballpoint pen factory just to support herself (barely). She didn't much care for the job, but it paid for a cheap apartment, and once she'd settled in she started scouting for sources of income that were better suited to her tastes.

"I realized I could live anywhere, if I was willing to do anything it took to earn a living," she said. She began by learning how to do carpentry and wiring by assisting the local handyman who was often a bit unreliable. "I saved his job for him, and started bringing in more renovation business by hanging out with home owners whose primary residence was in the States and talking up our services.

"Once there was a hurricane, and while everyone else was diving under their tables I rolled out of bed, went downtown and bought a chainsaw! I knew a lot of people were going to need trees removed from their property within 24 hours, and I was ready."

After everyone in the small community got to know her, she began house sitting a mansion, and now her domicile is whichever vacation home she's been hired to take care of while the owners are gone. If you have a way to prove you're trustworthy and reliable, you too might be able to house sit for a millionaire. There's a magazine dedicated to finding that kind of gig at *caretaker.com*, but I get mixed reports about it. The best way is to establish yourself in the community and start doing household repairs like she did.

If you know in your heart where you want to live, that's a very big thing. A lot of people haven't figured that out, so you're one of the lucky ones. See if you can find a way to spend some time there, as often as possible, before relocating. Get to know the ropes. Hang out with the people who have to earn a living. Start thinking about what services are needed and a plan will start brewing in your mind.

Money, how to subsidize your dream

There's a difference between doing what you love for money and financing what you love to do. Often it's a good idea to find some way to bring in money that has nothing to do with what you love, allowing you to develop your dream without the pressure of having to make it profitable.

However, the grind of a regular job isn't for everyone. Instead of a 9–5 job, you might consider finding a number of small revenue sources to pay your bills.

Multiple Revenue Streams

Setting these up for yourself is a great idea. It means you take part-time jobs or sell your services in a number of ways at the same time, so that together they bring in enough income for your expenses. You don't have to worry about getting bored, and if one source of money dries up, you still have three or four more. That can be very soothing to your sense of security.

STEP ONE:

Check the classifieds—they show what sorts of services are needed in your location. You can answer them and try for a job, but a better way might be to offer the same service on your own, without being hired. You can also figure out how to offer a service that will help the employer who placed the ad, and/or how to offer a service to help the people who might answer the ad.

Flip through the yellow pages—they give you ideas of what you can do on your own. As a fun little exercise, pick a letter in the yellow pages and see which of the services listed you could do on a small scale: (A — Aquarium Services "I could clean aquariums in my neighborhood." Auto repair "That's out, no talent there, but what if I offered a service for finding the best rates for auto repair, acting as a broker, through the internet? Or what if I persuaded a garage to do overnight tune-ups? I could bring the car in at night, and return it all fixed up in the morning.")

STEP TWO:

Take an inventory of your assets—You've got all kinds of tools for bringing in extra money, but it may have been a while since you had a look at them. Try out these suggestions and see what shows up:

1) List what you loved as a kid (were you a math whiz? did you love bikes?)

2) List anything you're good at (be very objective here: what comes easily to you? what have people told you were your talents?)

3) List anything you've been paid to do (that includes work done for friends or family—don't list job titles; try to think of exactly what you were being paid for)

4) List all your personal resources (van? computer skills? a foreign language? theater or mechanics knowledge? lots of free time? extra money? an extra room or apartment?)

5) List your ancillary skills (organizing? leading? good with people? selling? kids? learning? researching? teaching? brain-storming?) (See "A" for Ancillary skills)

6) Find local problems, wishes of homeowners and renters, or stores and customers or parents or pet-owners. Think of ways to make things better. What could you do to help schools, commuters, businesses, car owners, students?

Look at your list, then look at those want ads once more to see if you can find a match of some kind. What do the ads indicate that people in your community need and that a clever person like you can provide (without actually taking a job)? Try out one or two ideas on a small scale while keeping your present job. If you like the results, add a few more. See what happens.

Money, ways to make quick cash

This is so much fun I gave it a chapter of its own (go right to "Q" for Quick Cash).

Money, create a nestegg for your dream

Matt worked as a legal proofreader for six months every two or three years, and used the money to subsidize living overseas in the Greek isles. Dan works as a summer forest service employee to finance his life in Italy. If you dedicate all the funds from a certain kind of activity—say you use every penny you make cleaning apartments to buy the sound equipment you need—you're building up a nestegg. It's easy to come up with ingenious, low-risk ways of making some extra money and using it only for your dream.

Mailing List

There are two things you have to do if you want to work for yourself and survive:

1) Make a promotion schedule, and

2) Never stop looking for good names to put on your mailing list.

One of the very best things about modern technology is that you can send an email to your whole list without printing up something or licking a stamp. If you have a mailing list, you can send a message to your people any time you like. It costs next to nothing and they won't throw your message into the trash if they recognize your name. You need a mailing list if you're going to use most of the self-employment ideas mentioned in this book, such as selling something on the internet, inviting people to an event, or announcing what exotic dish you'll be cooking at the next meeting of your dinner club.

Buying a list is an option if you have something special to sell to a specific group like nurses or teachers; it's worth your while to buy the email list for those groups. But in most cases, you want your mailing list to consist of "fans"— people who know the quality of your work and want to be informed of what new, exciting things you're up to. You can announce a telephone class or a new product or your new book by writing a short email note with a link to your website and sending it to your whole list. Nothing has done as much to level the playing field between the well-heeled and regular folks without much money as email lists and links to the internet.

How do you build a mailing list? You can give one-time, free seminars and make sure everybody who attends puts their name and email address on your sign-up sheet. With that mailing list, you have a business. Now the question is, "how do you get people to come to these seminars?" Well, you can start a grapevine or e-vine by asking people to invite their friends. You can also make an announcement on Craigslist.com, open a special interest group on meetup.com, or get some business to allow you to run a program on their premises—preferably something that will get them some sales—and let them have the job of bringing in people. You can also do a free seminar for a church and let them publicize it in their newsletter, as I did for All Soul's Church in Manhattan when I ran an Entrepreneur's Workshop for them. Of course, you can also use good old press releases and flyers to bring people in.

IMPORTANT NOTE: Building a mailing list doesn't mean you use any of the following ideas only once. Or five times. You do them over and over, in a cycle, and you never stop doing them. Pace yourself, give it a few hours a week if you're busy, but never stop building your mailing list. It's the basis of almost every business (and of *every* internet business).

SIX WAYS TO BUILD A GREAT MAILING LIST

1) **Get PR**

Get yourself on the radio or in a local newspaper and give out your website address, or your email address (and make it *easy to remember!* Not everyone has a pencil handy). Make it interesting to visit your website. For example, invite people to send in questions to which they'll find answers, like my friend Gustav the food coach did (he's under "C" for Coach).

2) **Find reviewers**

If you're planning to sell some service or product for pets, for example, find the magazines dedicated to pets and read the columnists and book reviewers. At the bottom of each column is their email address. They want to hear from you because they have a column to fill up for every issue. And they'll be pleased to be on your mailing list and receive emails from you—especially if your emails are "sexy". For example, "Every Poodle's best kept secret!" (For ideas, check out the covers of any major magazine and you'll see their teasers, the ones that make you eager to look inside.)

3) **Speak in front of groups**

You can create a list by speaking in front of groups of people from different organizations and asking them to give you their email addresses so you can notify them of any future appearances. Ask them to toss their business cards or email addresses into a fishbowl to be on your list and to get a prize in a drawing. Take the names home and enter them after the event is over.

4) **Hand out bookmarks or flyers** that invite people to come to your site (give them a good reason to come, like a helpful, free bulletin board), and once there have a button that invites them to sign up for your mailing list.

5) **Write a letter to an editor of a magazine** and sign your name and email under the letter. If you're published, you may get emails from people who read your letter, and their return addresses go into your mailing list.

6) **Offer to write an article** (or a column) for an e-zine or your local newspaper and make sure your name and website or email address are very prominent.

REMEMBER: the best kind of mailing list is one you assemble from people who have seen you speak or read something you wrote or came to your website and asked to be on your list. Make it your ongoing project to build an up-to-date list of email addresses and you'll never regret it.

N

Niche, find one

This one is important, so it's really worth taking some time to think about. If you are able to find a need that isn't being met, you've got a business on your hands. Start with something you know is needed, or something you enjoy doing—say training dogs or creating scrapbooks or doing closet makeovers or driving people long distances—and find a market by tailoring this service to one segment of the potential population. Create online books for stamp-collectors, train dogs to play outfielder for baseball devotees, drive Christians or Croatians to reunions, do closet makeovers for kids or retirees or left-handed people, etc.

If you can find a niche, you'll get a lot of repeat business, and if your niche is interesting enough, you can get lots of publicity, too. Two brothers from Greece did that in my neighborhood. They set up a warm, friendly food market specializing in super-fresh produce and home-style takeout meals, and they chose a location directly across the street from a huge supermarket chain store. To everyone's surprise, they do a booming business, and have been written up in the neighborhood newspaper more than once.

Where to begin? Well, aside from your own neighborhood, the obvious place is the internet. Start looking at Newsgroups and Newsletters/Listservs that are of interest to you (see "Newsgroups" below). You will find a lot of information about what's currently out there. I did a fascinating search on www.liszt.com and found a place where one can find any listserv and/or create their own for free!

When you think you've hit on something and can identify who you want your market to be, send out press releases to the appropriate magazines and newspapers and e-zines on the net, including all your information and a statement about how your business will help your market. That could launch your business right away!

Newsgroups

When people want to talk to other people with the same interests, they go to "Usenet newsgroups". Finding your people can make a tremendous difference in your life. In fact, it can be the difference between achieving your dreams and giving up on them. There's nothing in the world that makes your dream feel as legitimate as being in the company of people who respect it. And nothing will help you achieve it more than people who know the ropes and are willing to tell you what they know. So every time you start feeling proud of being a "loner" who doesn't join anything (an attitude I had myself for many years), hit your forehead with the heel of your hand and say "Cut it out!" (if you want your dreams to come true, that is).

But it can be tricky to navigate your way around Usenet newsgroups. At this writing, there are already close to a million different discussion groups, from "shyness" to "marriage" to "unschooling". For a good start, head over to *www.google.com,* click on "groups" and do your best to plug in key words that might help you find your people. You might need some time to locate all the newsgroups it would be useful to know, but you only need to find them once and then you can settle into the lovely feeling of being surrounded by people who understand and want to help you. You'll get a lot of pleasure and build your confidence when you start helping them, too.

Spinoff idea: If you've got time and surfing Usenet is your idea of fun, why not offer a valuable service by helping others find their relevant newsgroups? They can answer a questionnaire on your website or just send you an email telling you their problem. Maybe they need a good dentist for their Yorkie, or they think they just found a page of the Dead Sea Scrolls in their great aunt's attic. You can do a preliminary search and give them an estimate of what you might be able to find for them, and how much it will cost. If you're good and fast, you can keep your prices relatively low and still earn a great hourly wage. Come on my bulletin board to show off a little and let people know where they can find you. The word will get out. (This is a great idea for an income stream. That is, it might not earn you all the money you need, but it might earn 15% of it and then you can do lots of other things in addition. I love income streams. They keep life interesting.)

Newsletter/Listserv

You know what a newsletter is, and you can write and print one or send an email newsletter to your emailing list (which you will build and that's an order! If you skipped around in this book, head back to "M" for Mailing List and you'll get lots of tips for gathering a lovely mailing list for yourself.) But what I'm suggesting is a very different kind of newsletter. It's sometimes called a listserv. Yes, that's spelled right, no "e" at the end. A listserv is a fine thing, indeed. Some people call it a "list" or a "mailing list" but that's not quite right, either. I'm not a techie, but I was so astonished when I saw a listserv in action that maybe I'm the right person to try to explain it to those among you who aren't techies, either. Here goes:

Imagine you had an email list of a whole bunch of people who were animal lovers or, even more specifically, a group of people who were interested in the breeding of alpacas and who had all signed up to be on the mailing list of a website about alpacas. And supposing you wanted them all to get a message from you. You could write an email, send it to the address they provided with the push of a button and everyone on the list would get your question in their email inbox. Suppose you said "I hear a new breed of alpacas is coming into North America from Peru. Does anyone know anything about this?"

Everyone on your mailing list would get that question as an email in their inbox. No big deal. That's a nice way to send out a newsletter (and that's why listservs are sometimes combined with newsletter discussions.)

The amazing thing would happen if any of the recipients chose to answer. If one person hit his Reply button and said, "Yes, I saw 2,000 of them, dark brown,

146

walking in a huge herd across the border at Texarkana," (you know I'm making all this up, right?) that response would go into the email inbox of everyone on your list too!

That's new. It means every time anyone on the lists asks or answers anything, you'll know about it. You'll get an education you can't buy in any school. And while you can't advertise a business or a service on a listserv, every time you answer a question in a truly helpful or knowledgeable way, you'll get noticed. If you sign each answer with your name and your company name and address, people will be able to find you. It's a really nice way to increase your business, and to know what your people's concerns are.

It's also a great way to build a community, or keep in touch with one, that could otherwise melt away. Just set up a listserv and invite some old buddies from the Peace Corps or college to sign up (and to contact whoever they know in the group to join, as well). What we're talking about is checking your email before you go to sleep and finding a note from someone wonderful you thought you'd never find again. Nice. You should do it.

(To start your own listserv, go to liszt.com/create/index2.html. Listservs were free last time I looked.)

Night Out!

If you're someone who always knows what to do with a free evening, it means you have a talent and can make it work for you. If you established yourself—either at work or any organization you belong to—as a Night Out expert, you could arrange events like theater tickets or swing dancing. You can scour all the weeklies for events and tailor an evening for couples or groups—or singles! Never overlook the singles market for evening activities. You can include ethnic dining with live music (or belly dancing!), a comedy club or open choir practice for Händel's Messiah (a lot more fun than it sounds). If you feel like expanding, you can start a hard copy newsletter and hand it out at super markets so people will call you, or offer an email newsletter on your website. That's just one step away from an entertainment publication.

Nightmare Nights!

If you love mystery or horror, you can find the most haunted-looking house in your town and conduct recreational evenings where people pay to have the living daylights scared out of them (see the first spinoff idea under Love Consultant in "L" for more ideas). Corporations hire professional companies to do this and pay serious money for the privilege, but until you've done it on your own and gotten some articles or good reviews in the papers, they might not be interested. Anyway, you need to start small to see if you can do it.

You don't have to buy the house, of course. Just rent it for the evening from the owner—and if they still live there, that's fine, too. They can act as your experts, showing you all the hidden places, squeaky stairs and creaking shutters, as well as joining in and helping to scare everybody.

Nostalgia

Anyone who knows what kind of car James Dean drove in "Giant" or loves the sound of a jukebox picking out a 45 and playing it (scratches and all) is a nostalgia expert. Don't listen to people who think you've frittered away your time, because someone wants your services (or could be made to see that they do.) Did you know that restaurants pay people to go picking through flea markets and going-out-of-business sales for nostalgia to hang up on their walls? If you've been to any newly built 50's-style diner, you know what I'm talking about. There are tons of ways to make money as a memorabilia expert or collector or consultant.

You could decorate homes or halls for parties or consult for the movies. If you're the kind of person who annoys your friends during a film by saying, "No one wore *that* kind of hat in the 50's!" Hollywood might need you. Or you could come up with wonderful "Junk Events" where people dress up in vintage clothing, maybe drive vintage cars to a location where they could have a vintage swap meet (and you could provide the vintage music and portable dance floor!) Yes, you would charge for admission, have a drawing, have a contest for the best something-or-other, sell nostalgic food. And you would announce it in your local newspaper's events column, announce it to your mailing list and try to talk on the radio or get an article written about you in the local paper. You could also start a newsletter and get advertisers who sell all things nostalgic. Or you could start a catalog of memorabilia catalogs. And, of course, there's good old eBay.

I saw a piece on TV not long ago about a man who collected videos and films of the first TV commercials. He had videos of black and white 1953 Buick ads and Stepford ladies in kitchens smiling brightly over their Crisco cans.

Hollywood pays him a lot of money to rent those videos these days. But you don't need to become a collector and rent storage space. You can combine this idea with "Night Out!" and have costume parties at a restaurant by age group: Wear What You Wore When You Were 15! (Maybe you can sell some of the clothing on your own site—or at the door of the party!)

There's really no limit to what you'll devise if you have a strong nostalgia gene. Sit down and look out a window. I'll bet you come up with five ideas in the next five minutes.

O

Ocularist

If you're an artist with a technical eye and an interest in medicine and/or helping people, you might consider being an ocularist. This is a trained painter who makes glass eyes. An ocularist makes the painted eye match the existing eye, which might involve a sitting with the subject, so the job requires a sensitivity for people as well as artistic ability. From what I've been told, the craft is learned through an apprenticeship. You can find out more at *www.albeye.com/albqeye.htm.*

If you're an artist with the slightest interest in medicine, see what other ideas you can come up with that use both. If you're a writer, do the same. I know of scholars in the field of Autobiography Studies who specialize in Medical

Autobiographies. See what you can come up with that pleases you, and then go looking for H-Levels.

Organizer

A professional organizer is someone who can organize anything—from your closets to your life. If they do their job right, you'll never lose another bill or another sock, and never miss another appointment. Sounds like heaven? Or are you one of those lucky people who *is* organized. If you are, you should provide this service for everyone else!

Ongoing Organizing services

Many organizing services say "Get organized once and for all." Do a search for "organize" on Google.com and you'll see what I mean. We know that disorganized people simply can't stay organized forever (just as we know there is no diet that you'll stay on for the rest of your life) but since that's the fantasy of the buyers, that's what people sell.

It might be a good idea to educate them to the realities. Advising that your program will last for a while and then they'll need your services again would make life easier for both you and your clients. Otherwise, every time you finish a job, you're out of work again. It's better for everyone concerned if your service is more like a gardener's than a bricklayer's. After visiting your client once and putting in the initial organizing effort, you'd know what their place looks like and where the problems are. If the client paid in advance (as they usually do with career coaches) they'd know an appointment was coming up and it would motivate them to take the next step. You could handle any problems that came up in your meeting.

Find a niche

I've been told there are organizers who specialize in cleaning up the acts of professional athletes and models or people with Attention Deficit Disorder (I wish one lived in my spare room!) They speak in front of parents groups, teachers groups and to organizations dedicated solely to A.D.D. You could specialize in small businesses, or fashion designers, or event planners.

There are other things to organize if you've got the gift. You can offer your services to travel agents who handle business travelers, for instance. You could write a booklet (or an audio tour!) for them to offer their clients who travel every few days to another city and title it something like: "How To Bring Everything, Find Everything and Lose Nothing When You're in a Different Place Every Day."

You could get a lot of business by using that title for a speech you'd offer at travel agents' professional conferences, or the Junior League and gardening clubs all over the country for friends and spouses of business travelers. (You won't find many business travelers at the meetings because they rarely have the time.)

How about combining athletes and travel by starting an organizing service that specializes in athletic teams traveling from town to town? Or contestants and their families who go to beauty pageants? If you have superior organizing skills, there's absolutely no one who doesn't need you!

A well-placed ad (or story) in the right trade magazine—for example, an event planners magazine—might do you a world of good. Who would write the story? You can if you like, or call one of the writers on their masthead and suggest they write an article about "Ten Things An Event Planner Can Do To Always Be Perfectly Organized". (Change a few details and re-submit the article to a publication that serves managers and agents of actors, painters' reps, the bookkeepers for home business owners, or tax accountants! They'll send their clients to you!)

Online Classes

If you need or want to learn something but can't cut out enough time from your busy schedule to attend classes, you're in luck. Thanks to the wonders of the internet you can study almost any subject in your home, at midnight, if you like.

A search for "online classes" brought up the following entries (and dozens more):

1) LVS Online Classes — Web Design and Graphics Courses. Tutorials.

2) Hewlett-Packard Business Center — Online Classes

3) Third Age Learning Center — Free Classes

4) Genealogy.com — Genealogy Classes

5) eOnline Classes — universities and colleges directory

6) Online Classes — Joslin Diabetes Center (Free)

7) Online Writing Classes — Script Magazine (screenwriting class)

8) Classes in Electronic Poetry and Fiction offered by The New School Online University, New York.

The question you have to ask yourself is, if you could learn anything in the world, what would it be? What would you love to learn? And then, when you have the answer, ask one more question: Could you learn it online? Even if you prefer to be physically present in a classroom, an online class could get you started right away. The excitement could begin, not someday when you have the time and money, but now.

Check it out. Head over to google.com and start some searches for online classes. See what happens.

And since we're on the subject of online learning, how about this idea?

Teaching online

Take a look at *www.blackboard.com* for an impressive example of offerings from people just like you. Here's what their site says: "Blackboard.com guides you through simple steps for creating your online class, which is available immediately. If you can surf the internet, you can create a course Web site on Blackboard.com."

They host classes for schools, colleges and businesses all over the world and to my knowledge represent the cutting edge of virtual classrooms. (Things on the internet can change overnight, so don't hold me to this.)

What's handy about a place like *blackboard.com* is that you don't need to bring in the students. Blackboard will do it for you. It already has an impressive number of visitors, so your class will be seen. But if you don't mind bringing in your own students, if you've got the energy and focus to systematically gather addresses for your email list, you can offer classes yourself, on your own time, via email or telephone or Instant Messaging.

What should you teach? Anything you know and enjoy teaching. If you know more than your family cares to hear about the old days in Romania, including food and music and crafts, you can teach a class in it.

In fact, there are services where you can speak your lesson into a telephone and email people an address on the internet where they can go to hear what you said! (Go to *www.audblog.com*). Yes, you can arrange for them to pay you for the privilege, also online. (*Paypal.com* is just one example.)

Overseas

Living and working

If you're reading this book, chances are your English is pretty good. These days, that's like a ticket to ride: English teachers are in very high demand all over the world. If you have an adventurous spirit (and a little cash in your jeans to see you through sparse times), you might be willing to take your chances and in that case, you don't need to be certified. If you find yourself in any country that puts a high value on speaking English (Japan for instance), you can present yourself to a corporation or a department store that caters to tourists, or an English Language Coffee Bar (if you can't find one, you might consider starting one) and offer to teach conversational English.

You hear of a lot of college grads getting certified, however, because many schools that offer certification have a network that will almost guarantee you job placement anywhere in the world. I know an artist who was tired of working odd jobs to support her painting, and decided to invest in certification from a really good ESL (English as a Second Language) program and travel the world. In two years she's been to Italy, Mexico and now she's going to Prague. She pays for her own plane ticket, but knows she'll have a job when she lands. For more info about certificates and schools in your area, do an online search. You might also try these sites to get you started: *www.tesol.org,* *www.psrn.org,* *www.eslcafe.com,* and *www.eslincanada.com.*

Odd Jobs

Does the idea of going to an office every day turn you off? You may have thought until now that a mundane job was the only way to make money. Well, think again: here's a list of jobs you probably never considered (or even knew of) that people are doing right now. I've made a hobby of collecting oddball jobs in my travels by writing down every one I encounter. I speak to people on planes and in airports, in taxis and in restaurants and on the sets of TV stations. As you'll see below, my list of oddball jobs has been helped enormously by the people on my bulletin board, which I've tried to indicate throughout as best I can without interrupting the discussion. If anything below looks interesting to you, do a search on the internet. You'll be amazed. This list is just the tiniest glimpse at a world of work that goes on every day that we never hear about.

If you're having a hard time deciding what you might enjoy doing for a living, you can always find more like these. Just ask any group of friends to tell you the oddest jobs they know about. And while you're reading through this surprising list, keep your pencil ready so you can circle anything you like and write your H-Level in the margin. You might find out some unexpected things about what you love.

Curator of an odd museum

Someone on my bulletin board informs us that she has a friend who is the curator of the Jell-O Museum. Now, I didn't know there was a Jell-O Museum and I bet you didn't either. But if there's a Jell-O Museum, there are all kinds of museums we never thought of. So if you ever wanted to be a curator and thought museums were few and far between (or just too stuffy), maybe this could be an opportunity for you.

Of course, you can always start your own museum. People do it all the time, as you'll find if you take blue highways across the U.S. My family did that when I was a kid and we saw one-room museums with arrowheads and the skeletons of small animals in glass cases... well, never mind. There are fabric "libraries" that house scraps of fabric from long ago where designers do research and get ideas. And one of these days I'm going to raise enough money to create a small museum in a village in Central Turkey in an old restored home, just to keep alive some of the old ways that are passing away so quickly. I got the idea from an old house I saw in Corfu, Greece, created by the father of a friend, full of artifacts, embroidered linens on the beds. It was quiet and beautiful and filled my head with ideas.

Is this odd activity of being a different kind of curator stirring any H-Levels over 7 in you? I haven't heard it brought up much in career books, at least not in any way that feels warm and personal. Thought I'd throw it in, just in case it's one of the things that makes your heart beat a little faster—as it does to mine.

Want to hear some more odd jobs?

You can create **floral arrangements out of candy**, like a shop called "Candy Blossoms". This is also the primary industry of a lovely town in the hills of Italy called Sulmona. As soon as you get off the train from the lowlands you're looking in the windows of shops filled with every kind of candy structure, mostly made from sugar-coated almonds (called, oddly enough, "confetti"). If you'd like to be a first-rate **candy sculptor**, you might want to visit Sulmona and take some photos of yourself in that setting for your press kit. You'll definitely get instant cache and if you speak Italian you might get some great tips, too! Take a pencil and sketchpad and even if no one talks to you, you'll get dozens of ideas just from looking in all the shops.

Here's more from my bulletin board:

> "On www.guru.com I found an ad for a **Seafood Taster**, for a San Francisco seafood company. It pays $22 an hour for 8 weeks!"

> "My cousin lives in Whitehorse, Yukon Territory and works for a government agency that provides **satellite mapping** info to mining companies, fishermen, hunters, etc. She used to run fishing charters and her husband operated a **helicopter adventure company**—dropping campers into wild terrain and coming to get them again in a week."

> "Two women I know **operate apple orchards** and there are several women in our area who run CSA farms (Community Supported Agriculture)— coops where people buy a share in the spring, work some on the farm, and get weekly harvest baskets all summer and fall."

> "Around Valentine's Day a radio station interviewed a guy who helps people **plan marriage proposals.**"

> "There's a company in town that will rid your backyard of your dog's doody. If that doesn't gross you out, you've got work, because there's obviously a big demand."

> "My cousin's daughter, who loves the outdoors, now works as an outfitter for a **fly-fishing adventure company** just for women, called 'reel women'."

> "Heard of this woman, Isabelle Tihanyi, from California who started **The Surf Diva School** and is quite successful at it. So basically she spends her days on the beach, gets to travel, meet people, does women a great service and earns good money. Try surfdiva.com for ideas and details!"

"I have a cousin who **makes black powder rifles and accessories**. I have another friend (several, actually) who are **professional armorers** and **sword-makers**."

"I have worked as an **auction coordinator** (maybe contact the National Auctioneer Association www.auctioneer.org)."

"My husband worked as a **nude model** for the college's theatre class (costume design). They were looking for men with 'real' bodies and it paid fairly well. Try the art department of your nearby university."

"My brother, a scuba diver himself, knows a guy in Florida who makes a good living **scraping barnacles** off the bottoms of boats for a hefty fee. It costs boat owners oodles of dough to have the boat dry-docked to have this done, and it is much cheaper to have a scuba diver do it."

"I know a '**beer taster**'. He was employed by a beer distributor and his job was to go from bar to bar, tasting the product. If you're looking for a similar job, check out beer distributors in your town."

There are people who do **sign-language on stage** for the audience during the performance of rock bands, and even rappers! To find out about training, look at the American Sign Language site: *www.accd.edu*. You can read about Ben & Jerry's **Flavor Development Specialist** (Professional Ice Cream Taster) at *http://outtakes.com/work/taster.html*. It's possible to be a facilitator who helps people **swim with wild dolphins.** *www.swimmingwithdolphins.com* might lead to more information. If you'd like to be a professional **sandcastle builder** take a look at *www.sandyfeet.com*.

St. John's cathedral in New York brought over **master masons** from Italy to teach their art to apprentices from local schools. You can volunteer to help and work on a Cathedral just like they did in the middle ages. Toss a skill like that over your shoulder and you can march to any town that needs beautiful stone work. You'll have to let them know you're there but once you've inspired them with your portfolio and pointed out the buildings that could benefit from your craft, you won't have much competition.

There are also people who work only as **conference staff**, and move from conference to conference. They don't do the planning part of the conference, just the onsite logistical details at each location. Contact a conference center like the Javitz Center in New York to see what's available. At a waterfront park there are people who get paid to let their dogs run on the beach a few times a day to **keep the geese away**. Nice job for the owner and fun for the dogs, too. Check out the city parks in your town and see what jobs are listed. The inner workings of our city parks are an unknown world to most of us and you can be sure there are odd jobs all over it.

I saw an ad recently for a **Mystery shopper**: the job was to go to certain stores, buy things and evaluate the service, store presentation, attitudes among staff and report back to the owner/head of the store: www.gofeedback.com or *www.mysteryshop.org*. There was another kind of "mystery" job I saw, for major hotel chains. It involved traveling all over the country (and the world), sleeping in major hotels. There was a long list of things to do, like ordering meals at odd-hours from room service, having your suit cleaned and pressed, using the health club, etc. There were checklists to be filled out, too, on things like whether there was an extra pillow in the closet, or rolls of toilet tissue. (Nice job if you like to travel.) *www.hoteljobs.com* might have more information. And yet another mystery job: Students, actors, or anybody who wants part-time work with a very flexible schedule and good pay should look into being a **"Mystery Guest"** for any of the major fast food restaurants. You're actually a quality control person, checking to see if the restaurant is run well. Contact the big chain restaurants for more information.

A woman in her late 60's, a retired home economics teacher near Albany, NY, **bought a farm**, fixed up a commercial kitchen in a converted barn, and is luring tourists, scouting groups and others onto the farm: They can work in the farm gardens or buy already-harvested produce, then cook and can it in her kitchen and take home their own home-made jellies, jams, pies, breads, etc.

Spinoff idea: Wouldn't it be a wonderful odd job to **offer a service to small farmers** helping them find ways to earn additional income so they could keep their farms? You'd locate the farm, check out what the owners might be willing to do, such as:

1) Have guests for home stays.

2) House families who'd like to spend their vacation with their children farming and caring for farm animals.

3) Instead of a semester abroad, why not hold a "semester on the land" for parents who don't want their kids to travel abroad these days?

4) Set up a computer-training center and/or a 'help center' and bring new jobs to the area as well as income to the farmer.

5) Bring in assisted living people for short or long stays.

6) All of the above.

And when you find what the farmers might be comfortable doing, you go out and find the talent (teachers, cooks, theater groups, etc.) and, of course, the customers by any means of marketing that seems appropriate: placing notices in the nearest big city's events columns, writing articles in national magazines (or getting a freelance writer or someone on the masthead to write them) and doing internet marketing of all kinds.

You could travel all over your state (or every state, if you decided to create a national organization), finding farmers in need and matching them up with fascinating, talented people who'd love to run a program at their farms. I don't know how you'd get paid for this, but some options that come to mind are these: you can take a percentage of the tourist's fees or become a non-profit 501(c)(3) organization and/or get some kind of grant (from the U.S. Department of Agriculture? FarmAid?) Go to your local Foundation Library (you'll find it on the internet) and ask the librarian for some help. Or better yet, get sponsors from the people who sell to farmers: feed stores and tractor shops who want people to know they care about the small family farm. See if they'll help you finance this idea. You'll do well if you gather together a nice, fat mailing list so you can send stories and photos out to the world to let them know how great a farm visit could be (see "M" for Mailing List).

P

Part-time Dreams

People usually assume that their dreams have to be all or nothing—which is why a lot of dreams never seem to get off the ground. But if you could make your dream part-time, imagine all the energy and pressure you'd save: you could start right away and later think of ways to make it more full-time if you wanted.

Victoria's part-time coffeehouse

Victoria wants to own a coffeehouse/theater and wants it to be a theatrical school to boot, teaching everything from acting to set production and playwriting. She knows experts who would be happy to teach the classes if she could provide a location; but she can't imagine how she'll get the money to own or rent a space suitable for a coffeehouse/theater or where she'll get the time to run the place full-time. However, if she reframes her dream into part-time, at least temporarily, she can use someone else's space and do the whole dream almost right away. Here's how:

1) Victoria can have the acting classes every Monday during the day at a nearby coffeehouse which is usually closed Mondays. The owners are quite enthusiastic about her plan.

2) If her schedule allows it, she can learn how to run a coffeehouse by working or even "interning" there. It's worth the investment of her time because she'll know if it's really what she wants, and the experience will be priceless. (She has to try to help out in the office as well as on the floor with customers so she really understands the business.)

3) She can run set design classes at a local community college, but she favors a lumber yard/module furniture store in the downtown area of her town and is trying to get permission from the owner. If he can do it he should, because it would bring him more customers from the students and if he contacts the local newspaper about holding set design classes there, he has a good chance of getting some publicity, too. Since he closes at 6 pm, the classes can be done in the evenings without getting in the way of his daily business.

4) Victoria knows an independent performing group that would be thrilled to present plays during the week as soon as she invites them, which will also bring in business for the coffee shop.

5) She can forget about the coffee shop setting entirely and do the whole project, from acting classes to set design to performances (and even serving great coffee) in different people's homes! Or in a truck on the road, as a traveling theater workshop with refreshments all ready to go!

Party Motivator

Some people just have a natural gift for bringing life to social events. Everyone knows the difference between a great party and dead one, and every host dreads the latter. So, if you know what it takes to make people really enjoy themselves, your skills are in big demand and you can turn them into income. This was on National Public Radio:

> "Suzy Choy loves to have a good time, and she's found a way to get paid for it. Choy is a 'party motivator'. Her job is to make sure guests have fun at the weddings, bar mitzvahs and corporate events she's hired to attend." (Here is the link to the audio file: *www.npr.org/rundowns/segment.php?wfId= 1490273*)

Is there some part of this idea that gets your H-Levels up above a 7? Take that part, redesign the rest of the idea to suit your tastes and see what you come up with. (How about sitting in the bleachers at kids' practice ball games and cheering their efforts to keep their spirits high? Or bringing a group of friends to applaud the performance of a stand up comic? Cruise ships are certainly looking for you if you're like Suzy Choy.)

Be a Peddler...on a bike!

A peddler is someone who sells things. Or it's someone who peddles along on a bike. Or both. In Austin TX there's a soup peddler who delivers soup to over 100 people. Incidentally, he quit his corporate job to do this and has never looked back. Maybe you can develop a different kind of business using this model. What else could you deliver besides soup? Take a look at his website. It's fun: *www.souppeddler.com*. And for more ideas, see "B" for Business on a bike.

Prepare taxes

For the right person this is an ideal job. Think of it: you work the three or four months of tax season like a beast, and then you have the rest of the year off. It isn't a pipe dream. I know people who do it. One of them not only bought and restored his own brownstone in Brooklyn, but is always looking for interesting things to do the rest of the year. If you hate the idea, forget it. You won't do a good job. But if you're detail-oriented and fairly good with numbers, you might actually have a good time! (I heard an accountant speak a few years ago who said that tax accounting for her clients was utterly fascinating: "You know so much about them, it's like reading a novel or a biography. You even know their secrets!") If writing Romance novels is the dream you're subsidizing, this could be a wise source of income for you. You'd never run out of ideas. (And you could travel to Capri and write that novel with the extra time and money you'd have.)

If you specialize in doing the taxes of people who do what you do or did (law or corporations, performing, art, photography, home repair or dog-walking) you'll find your people without too much trouble: they're the people you know. And finding a specialist will make them very happy.

How do you learn to become a tax preparer? H&R Block used to train people for a minimal fee so you'd work for them (which I would do at first, if I were you. The experience is very valuable.) But so many people trained and left to start up their own services that I think they've wised up by now and might charge more than before. Check it out. You can specialize in micro businesses by reading one of my long-ago favorite books, *Small Time Operator* by Bernard Kamoroff. Apparently I'm not the only person who loves that book. It's always in print and has been updated frequently.

To start earning money soon, you can stay with Block or work for another tax preparer—or two. How would you find them? Reach out your hand in any crowded elevator and you're sure to touch people who personally know one.

Publishing

e-books

You don't have to get involved with e-book companies or costly software to publish your own e-book, and your readers don't need to own a special reader apparatus. Their computer will do just fine and here's how: In many word-processing programs (Microsoft WORD for example) you only need to push one button to turn your document into a lovely book. It's called "Adobe PDF" and it's not important what that stands for as long as you know how to use it. It provides you with professional-looking pages and a lovely table of contents that helps readers move around in the document. And, unlike going through the hassle of getting hard copies printed up at a professional printer, the price is right. Once you own the software (mine came bundled with my new computer), we're talking about zero dollars in publishing costs.

Hard copy books

On the other hand, if you're someone who wants to hold your book in your hand and see it on *amazon.com,* that's not expensive anymore either. Just use the services of reputable Print On Demand publishers like *xLibris* or *iUniverse.* You can see their ads in Writer's Digest Magazine, or look up 'self publishing' on the internet. I'd advise having some of your books in hard copies if you want to be a speaker. Even if you don't sell them, you can include them in your press kit and impress the people who receive it.

Q

Quick Cash

I'm not talking about finding work you love, or even saving up a nest egg for your dream. The ideas here are for those times you need to make some money fast and you don't mind doing work you're not in love with. Basically, we're talking about doing something once, or occasionally. Either way, it's a good idea to get your contacts for this kind of enterprise set up well in advance. If any ideas below seem possible and tolerable to you, arrange to do them at least once before you really need to. Don't assume they'll work until you've done that. (You'd be amazed at what can go wrong when you're desperate.) Here's a list of quick money makers from my bulletin board, friends on the telephone and the dark recesses of my own mind. Some are better thought through than others, but they should give you something to work with. Let me shoot them past you quickly, but don't forget to circle anything interesting, even if it's only one word, and write your H-Level in the margin.

1. Be a substitute teacher

The education board of every city or town should have a website—in New York City it's www.teachny.com—or at least accessible offices, where you can post your resume and inquire about substitute teaching possibilities. You do not have to be certified to substitute, though different boards may have different requirements. The day ranges from actually doing another teacher's lesson plan to giving out tests and reading a magazine or teaching an inspired class if you've got it in you. (This is the Quick Cash section, so we're not being as fussy as usual.)

2. Model nude for art classes

Contact local schools with art departments and give modeling a try well in advance of the time you actually need cash. You need to find out how much they pay and if you can hold still long enough to qualify. They need real people of both genders and all sizes and shapes so don't fret about imperfections.

3. Dismantle booths at trade shows

Visit booth owners towards the end of a trade show and offer to help them take the booth apart and haul it away. Look at this heartfelt plea for help from the Angel Ladies on my bulletin board:

> "This weekend we're doing a trade show, and I'm dreading it already. Setting up the booth is fine, we're still fresh and excited. But taking it down! By Sunday evening, we'll have been on our feet for thirty or more hours and 'on' with booth visitors. At that point, the idea of repacking stuff, hauling it to the van, and loading it is simply overwhelming. More than once, when the show ended, all I wanted to do was crawl under the skirted table and sleep, not take down the booth. If someone came by and said, 'Hey lady, I'll pack and haul this stuff for you for $50,' I'd have given $75!"

Try visiting shows and handing out brightly colored flyers, or go around to the booths around closing time to see who could use your services.

HURRY UP SERVICES

The next entries are for impromptu work. Your clients have to know about you before they need you. And you need to be ready to drop everything and go to them when they call. I'd even try to set up a mailing list and write them every few weeks to remind them that you're available. If you have backup people you can rely on, you'll never get caught short; but they have to be reliable, maybe even bondable. If you get people with a wide array of skills, you just might have a very special kind of employment agency. That's not quick cash for you, just for the people who work for you—and you might like the work very much. (You'd better, because this kind of work doesn't go away. You can't strand people who think you're going to jump forward when they need you.)

Here are some of the things you (or your backup people) might think of covering:

4. Impromptu animal sitter

What happens if you're leaving town and the person who watches your dog suddenly disappears? It's happened to me, and what a nightmare it was! I ended up taking my dog with me and running a four-hour workshop with him on my arm! There was no other way. Some people weren't thrilled (like the rather proper ladies who brought me in to speak) but I had no choice. I couldn't leave my loveable but weird little dog with just anyone or I'd have been courting disaster. (He's very small but gets all fierce with every size dog and could get himself in a lot of trouble. My pet sitters have to be ready to protect him from getting his just desserts at any moment.) How I wish I'd known someone reliable who could solve my last-minute crisis! To advertise, put up flyers at pet supply stores and veterinarians and don't forget to get listed on *www.craigslist.com.*

You can also offer emergency pet sitting for out-of-towners traveling to your location. Contact travel agents, airline ticket offices and hotels, and tell them about your service. Show them references. (You should be able to get one from your veterinarian.) If the hotel doesn't allow pets, offer to bring the pet to your home and they might be very happy to tell their guests well in advance.

5. Prepare a week's dinners in someone's home

"I'd be so happy to have someone come by and cook up dinners I could freeze. I think I'd pay serious money to have five casseroles or whatever in the freezer," I was told by a very busy software designer who wants to eat right. You might have to stop by a market to pick up the necessary food (and storage cartons), cook all night, and deliver the food first thing in the morning before your client leaves for work, but some people don't mind emergencies and even enjoy unpredictability. (It's never boring, you have to admit that.)

6. Match up outfits for busy (or colorblind) people

If someone were available to come over on the weekend and turn the closet into a place where each cluster of hangers held a perfectly matched outfit including shoes, belts, scarves, jewelry or cufflinks, some people would be so grateful. If you gained enough trust to visit some midweek, you could also check to make sure no buttons or shoelaces were missing and that everything was cleaned or polished and ready to go: you might become a very popular person. You'd need some flair and a bit of compulsiveness, but this wouldn't have to be your dream career or most important talent by any means.

7. Research, type, run to the printers

Find writers or students with looming deadlines who need last minute research or writing or typing. People in trouble will pay top dollar for someone fast and capable. Put flyers up in copy centers and markets near colleges, and call publishers or agents to let them know you're available to assist writers in a frenzy.

8. Do a one-time de-cluttering job for someone

I got this really helpful idea from my bulletin board:

"When my grandmother moved out of her huge home and into a retirement apartment, she had someone who specialized in interior design come and help her decide what should go with her and how she should arrange what she really wanted to keep. The designer also helped the family make distinctions between valuable antiques and things with solely sentimental value. I don't know how much the woman made an hour, but it was a lot, and she was worth it. It helped take so much of the emotional stress off, and people will pay a lot for that. My friend's great-uncle just died, and she would have been so grateful to have had someone to go through the basement and closets to get rid the junk and set aside anything valuable, like important papers or photos."

spinoff idea: If this sort of thing appeals to you and you're looking for a business of your own, you might consider heading up a whole group of rapid response helpers to dispatch to these sudden calls. You'd be the boss, and they would be reliable people who want to do the work. (They'd be able to say 'no' if necessary and it wouldn't be a problem if you had a big enough "stable" of good people to choose from.) Write up some flyers and call yourself something easy to remember, like Help in a Hurry, or Last Minute Assistant (or something better!) Then post those flyers, come up with some good stories of last-minute rescues you've executed and tell the local radio show (you can call in to local talk shows any time you like, and it's a great way to get known!); also tell newspaper and TV news shows all about it. Get in the phone book, and get a website up (a free one is fine) so you can be found easily. This is definitely the place for business cards with a magnetized back on them. If you're someone who can provide last-minute help for overwhelming tasks like those above, I'd like your name on the side of my refrigerator!

9. Perform for gatherings and crowds

Go to places like baseball games, car races, swap meets, expos or flea markets and perform for the crowd. You could juggle or clown around for the kids, play romantic guitar for couples, or write poems for $2 apiece.

Here's a list of some more places where crowds gather or people wait. See if you can add to it:

- train stations
- car races, horse races
- movie lines
- Dept of Motor Vehicles
- protest rallies
- parades
- traffic jams

And here are some random things you might consider doing there:

- make signs, decorate faces or t-shirts
- carry a small wireless setup computer and write emails for people stuck in traffic
- carry a charger and charge their cell phones and laptop computers
- hold someone's place in line so they can go sit down or get something to eat
- wash and/or lube people's cars while they're at a movie
- read palms or tarot or do astrology readings
- take dictation for letter writing

You can also provide services for helping the people who work at these places, by making change or watching the booth while they run out for a moment. Now, before the cash crisis hits, make yourself known to the regulars at these places so they're comfortable with you, and when you're in a pinch and need quick cash, they'll be glad to see you!

10. Sell something you own

It's human nature to accumulate things. But when those things stop being useful, they can be a burden. Why not sell them for quick cash? You'll be passing them off to someone who will appreciate them and clearing necessary space for your next dream.

Search your home (attic, garage, closets, car trunk) for things to offer on eBay or Yahoo or Amazon or Craigslist. You'd be amazed what people will buy! If it's in your house and you know you don't need it, the item is probably something that has sentimental rather than practical value. That's great, because you'll be able to write an affectionate description and everyone will want to buy it. Take a nice digital photo of your item, preferably against a contrasting background. Then head over to one of the above sites and ask them what to do next. eBay has a whole online program to teach you, and some of the others might have the same.

spinoff idea #1: sell for other people

If you discover an interest in this process that means you have a talent for it. And that means you can help your neighbors sell their stuff online for a percentage of the proceeds. The money will come to you so you're sure to get your cut. Just give them 75% of what comes in and you're even. Unless you're willing to keep their stuff at your place, and you don't mind post office lines, consider leaving the items at their house and let them do all the packing and shipping.

spinoff idea #2: teach online selling in your neighborhood

There are lots of people offering to teach how to sell online, and they're online themselves. The competition is steep. However, if you enjoy the process,

174

you can offer a workshop on it at a local adult learning organization. You'll make a little money for the class, but you'll also get a number of new clients who will want you to do the selling for them (even though you've shown them how). You'll be drawing in people who have heard about eBay and thought about selling online, but aren't computer literate or aren't comfortable with the process. People are curious about this subject and this is a low-threat way for them to examine it a bit closer. They'll ask you to help them for sure, if you tell interesting stories of online sales you did for other clients. That will give them the idea. Then be sure they have your email and telephone number so they can contact you in the future, after they take another look at an old brass lamp sitting in their garage and remember your stories.

11. Sell off those books you haven't opened in years

This question came up recently on my boards: "I have hundreds of books, some valuable, some not, in my house. I also have a closet filled with antique fashion magazines. How do I find places to sell these things?" Here's a sample of the answers this person got. I think you'll be as impressed as I was:

Head for these used book sites on the web:

www.amazon.com/exec/obidos/subst/home/home.html/002-6493057-5510617
www.alibris.com/cgi-bin/texis/searcher
www.keplers.com/
www.booksearch.com/request.html
www.auldbooks.com/biblio/asubs/
abaa.org/
www.scaruffi.com/fiction/booksell.html
shop.barnesandnoble.com/oopbooks/oopsearch
www.avenuevictorhugobooks.com/

"Here's another: You can find out what the value of your books and magazines are by searching eBay to see what similar items are selling for.

Also go to rare retail websites like *pbagalleries.com* to get an idea of high and low values for books....just fill in the blanks. When I'm selling a book or magazine, this is how I research."

12. Buy junky furniture at garage sales or flea markets, fix it and sell it on consignment or at flea markets or on eBay for many times what it cost you.

13. Do telemarketing for a week. This only works once. You'll never want to do it again.

14. Personally cater a special party, wedding or corporate function using personal contacts, relatives, or by asking another small caterer for overflow.

15. Design a website for a new business, or an existing one that wants to get online. (Step into your local cleaners or delicatessen and sell them on the idea!)

16. While you're at it, see if they'd like a newsletter (online or not) to remind their customers that they exist.

17. Open or close someone's pool or summer cottage or winterize their garden.

18. Trace someone's family tree and prepare an online presentation they can email to all the relations.

19. Sponsor a home party like Tupperware and get free merchandise which you can sell.

20. Tune up or repair a friend's car or major appliance.

21. Borrow and drive a friend's cab for the weekend.

22. Be a "Just in time" nanny-taxi: The pay can be good for someone who will drive kids to their activities.

23. Tutor college students: "The university campus where I teach has a number of tutoring jobs open, pays about $15 per hour, flexible scheduling."

24. Be an entertainer, storyteller or read Tarot cards for people at parties.

25. Offer a one-time service to small stores. Get things ready for them to do an inventory. Clean up after a display in their windows.

26. Be a production assistant to real estate agents: run out to find the right flowers or hang a special painting in a home that's for sale. Do the same for a window dresser by knowing the best places to find a purple feather boa or replica of the Titanic.

27. Find out what someone just doesn't want to do and do it for them. Is it balancing their checkbook, paying bills, making a difficult phone call or accompanying/delivering a difficult relative or a pet to another city? Doing the laundry or windows? Washing the dog? Do they want you to call them every day to tell them exactly what to eat so they'll stay on their diet? Or cook and deliver it for them?

28. Work for lawyers doing research, typing pleas, running documents down to the courthouse, etc. Don't wait for a job to be posted. Every successful lawyer is wildly busy. Convince them that you learn fast and can do the work almost at once. If you don't know what they want, do an informational interview with the office manager or legal secretary. Don't bother with big firms for this cold-calling stuff.

29. If you're in school you can often find unexpected on-campus jobs in the library, bookstore or cafe. Many schools give students one to two-hour shifts to accommodate class schedules.

30. Ask for little jobs around the college theatre or library that you can do part-time.

31. Check with student services and see if anyone needs a reader for students who might have problems with reading such as visual impairment or limited language skills.

32. Don't forget waitressing. That's how I got through college. You never go hungry (and neither do your friends!)

and if you don't mind driving or biking ...

33. Call a limo company and see if they'll keep you on backup for overflow.

34. Be a bike messenger. But don't forget, this isn't a way of life, this is for quick cash. Bike messengers have a hard (and dangerous) life.

35. Teach someone how to drive or ride a bike.

36. Take people to their appointments using their car (or yours, if you have one.)

and finally, some more miscellaneous ideas ...

37. Give pedicures in your home (or theirs). Or at retirement homes.

38. Contact moving supply stores and moving companies with a flyer: "if you wish someone would come over and pack everything you own, contact me."

39. If you're good at writing complaint letters to big corporations, do it for other people. It's a talent.

40. Throw a rent party

This is a good way to raise quick cash and it's been done by friends for friends for a long time. You don't have to pay the rent with the proceeds—you can take a trip to Catalonia instead—but these parties were originally designed to help friends pay the rent during times of duress. Everyone who comes pays $10 at the door, brings potluck food and a skill they can sell, like foot massage, palm reading, photo-taking, chess-instruction. You can have a contest, too. If one person knows some kind of trivia, you can have people throw questions at him or her. If they guess correctly, the questioner puts a dollar in the kitty. If they don't, the expert puts a dollar in the kitty. Speaking of the kitty, you can play poker too, but all the stakes go to the guest of honor, no matter who wins.

41. Sell your hair to a wig maker. You can also walk up to other people with long hair and offer to sell theirs for them.

42. Set up a food stand at a flea market and cook something good. Got an old recipe? Make it look nice on a piece of parchment paper and sell it. Only $1 if they buy a piece of pie.

43. Buy a bit of stage make-up and do children's face-painting in a mall, at a street fair or in the park. (Paint your own face first, so no-one will recognize you!)

44. Grow seedlings in pots in December and sell them in February when people are aching for spring. Include instructions.

45. Polish silver. Put up flyers, especially around the holiday season.

46. Baby sit on special holidays so you can charge more (I know someone who made $300 last New Year's Eve!)

47. If you can do basic knitting, try some long scarves in the colors of a local team and see if you can sell them to supporters.

48. Make fruit tarts/cheesecakes/mustard/preserves and sell to a local deli or diner.

49. Try selling raffle tickets for some item you're willing to part with. Where? Maybe at a rent party!

50. Ask relatives to give you cash instead of a birthday present later on.

51. Take a page from public TV and ask for a donation; then reward them with a gift, such as washing their car three times or performing at their next party...

(If you're not dizzy yet, head over to my bulletin board at *www.barbarasher.com* and enjoy yourself with hundreds more ideas for making quick cash.)

R

Radio

Here's a book you might not run into at your local bookstore:

> *Get Into Radio* by Robert C. Elsenpeter, 1998 Book World Services, Inc. Contact: 800-444-2524

The cover copy is very funny: "Don't go to Law School....Get Into Radio...Over 130 Internet Resources...Choose a Fun Career", and inside the author trashes lawyers and doctors while writing beautifully.

His Note to the Reader:

> "The purpose of this book is to entertain and provide information. This book is not subject to any outside governmental or legal review process. Neither is it a manipulative tool of the totalitarian Establishment, the hungry hounds of political correctness, or America's drab and sappy corporate media machine."

It's a good book. He tells you exactly what you need to know, including how to find a job opening and ace the interview. He also gives the addresses of Usenet newsgroups that will keep you up-to-date on the profession.

Retirement

For any of the ideas you read until now, were you thinking you'd consider it more seriously sometime in the future when you had more time? Or worse, are you waiting to retire so you that you can just sit in the sun and have complete freedom and rest? Listen carefully: Rest is for people who are ill or dead. Doing nothing is fine for Monday, but what about Tuesday? A good retirement doesn't mean complete bed rest, it means "no work you hate, plenty of work you love."

So get to work at once, only this time, make it work you love. If you don't know what that is, make *that* your project and start searching. It can be a fascinating project. Talk to anyone who looks like they're having a good time and find out why. Try to remember anything you ever enjoyed and try it again. If your retirement dreams include moving to another location, plan a visit and stay for as long as you can. Before packing up and relocating, you want to see if you like it as much as you thought you would.

But do not wait until you're free. Get so happily busy with something you can't wait until you retire so you can do more of it. Free time without a clearly defined role and something you have to and want to do every day can plunge you into a mood that makes everything seem impossible. Think about the word "retirement". At its root is the word "tire". That's what you're going to do without doing something you love. (It's also what you'll get around your waist if you just sit around!)

Trust me on this one. You'll be glad you did.

Research (see also "I" for Information broker)

If you like research, there are many ways to earn money that you'd enjoy. In law, for example, there are many online databases that contain what lawyers are always in need of on a daily basis—court decisions, statutes and regulations, and commentary on all of them. Rummaging efficiently or inventively through these databases on their behalf could provide you with lots of lawyer clients paying very decent fees for your services.

If you're someone who has an instinct for finding just about anything on the world wide web, there are other people looking for you as well. Here are some ways you can help them find you:

1) Create a website with an address that tells what you do (so search engines will find you easily) and then show a number of examples of the different kinds of research you do best.

2) Some people advise that you show your prices right on your site. You can put up your hourly fees (perhaps with a two-hour minimum) with special rates for very short jobs and other special rates for longer, more complicated projects (charge by the day—or a lower fee per hour). Find other researchers to get an idea how they handle their fee structure.

3) Pick the subjects you like best at first and see what comes your way. If you love any old kind of research, pick the kind that pays the most. If you find the field too competitive for a beginner, head in that direction and if you have a gift, you'll be as good as anyone after you've learned the ropes.

4) To find clients, have an Idea Party and ask everyone to help you think of all the kinds of people who might need help gathering information. You might find some unexpected and lucrative niches. Here are a few ideas to start with:

- Freelance writers could turn out a lot more work if you did their research for them. Journalists in newspapers or television news shows (the local ones might be more accessible at first) consume facts and stories voraciously.

- Grant writers come to mind. Any business of any kind or size needs information from dozens of trade magazines or good but not well known news sources on the net (like *www.asiatimes.com*, for example).

- Every department in every government agency, everyone who writes for textbook companies, even historical novelists who love to do their own research but are so addictive they're afraid they'll never get around to writing. (No kidding, I know one writer who says she's afraid to start researching because she'll never stop. She should turn it over to you!)

Of course, every student with a paper to turn in wishes you were a relative, but you may not feel it's right to do their research when that's one of the things they're supposed to be learning (and are getting graded on!) In that case, you can teach an online or telephone class on how to find facts and do their own research more efficiently.

Re-publish out of print books

If you love old books about some special subject—Sheep herding around the world or Antique motorcycles—you probably collect out of print books on the subject, and your small, personal library could be full of books others would love and don't even know about. You might want to re-publish these books. If the books are old enough, the copyright may have run out, but that might mean that the big publishers are reprinting them and that's tough competition. If they're not, contact the publisher or estate of the author (the internet should help you there) and ask if you can have the rights to republish them.

Recording

Do you have a flair for recording and taping and burning stuff on audiocassettes or CDs? Find out which conferences are coming to your area and contact the sponsoring association. See if they need anyone to record the speakers (and make duplicates) to sell to the audience when they leave (or to those who missed the lecture). You'll need a multi-recording device which is sold by companies on the net. I found them by searching for "sound reproduction".

Retreat!

If you'd love to teach, why not take it one step further and produce a retreat or a weekend workshop?

HOW TO START: What is your retreat for? *Who* is it for? How, as a retreat, does it take up more time and space than a regular class? If you were to run a quilters' retreat what would make it different from the Thursday night

Quilters' Group meetings? You'd have teachers and quilting bees and an exhibit. You might have people buying your quilts. Or selling them. In fact, you might be able to get companies that provide quilting supplies to pay for the whole thing. I spoke at a crafts conference years ago to hundreds of delightful crafters who made all kinds of things (including books on how to do crafts) and the sponsor was a large crafts supply manufacturer.

You can go as far as you like into any subject that matters to you. Leisure time—even meals—would revolve around the chance to meet so many like-minded people. A retreat creates a community. The possibilities are endless. This is such a jolly idea I think you have to stop and make another list, this time of all the subjects you can think of that could possibly be at the heart of a weekend retreat.

1. _____

2. _____

3. _____

4. _____

5. _____

6. _____

7. _____

8. _____

9. _____

10. _____

If you're really serious, assemble a committee. Have them help you get the word out and find people. You'll be sure to find them on the internet. Just do a search for your key words and you'll find web sites with mailing lists, and often with bulletin boards. Email the person who put up the website and talk to the people on the bulletin board to find out if they already have conferences and retreats—or if they wish they did.

Don't forget to get into newsgroups. These are discussion groups on every subject imaginable. On Google.com you simply click on "groups" and then do a search with a key word, like "quilting".

And don't overlook retreat centers themselves. They know which groups already do retreats and are goldmines of information on how to produce a retreat. And they're motivated to help you, because it means business for them. Your job is to figure out how many people need to sign up in order to meet your expenses and make some money for your time. Write out a plan. Have one person on your committee in charge of food, one in charge of tickets, one in charge of transportation.

How will you advertise? The same way you would for teaching—in trade magazines, specialized groups, bulletin boards (the ones in your office lunchroom or outside your supermarket and the ones the internet), and via email.

S

Stitcher

"Stitcher" is the androgynous term for seamstress and tailor. If you can sew, you can be a stitcher. There are many ways to use this skill, but if you only want to make a steady income, it isn't about making a three-piece suit or designing an evening gown—it's hemming pants and dresses, fixing tears, maybe taking in or letting out seams. Sometimes it includes restoration of vintage clothing, too. You could advertise for this job at the local laundromat and dry cleaners (as long as they don't have stitchers of their own). You could pick up garments, fix them while watching television in your own home, and then bring them back to their owner. It's a great way to make extra cash utilizing a skill so many people just don't have. Or you can turn it into a serious business. In New York we have someone called "The Ghost Tailor" who does alterations. It's a big city and you'd think there would be a stitcher on every block, but everyone who loves their clothes seems to know her name, and you have to wait in line to talk to her and show what you want when you visit her loft. (You could be the ghost tailor in your town—or neighborhood!)

More sewing ideas: Put up notices that you're available to sew at places where people repair sewing machines, and you might get someone looking for cottage industry-type stitchers. Also, post a notice at fabric stores, where designers can find you. And, as always, a nice flyer posted in the entries of grocery stores might bring in business.

You can also find people who sell vintage clothing and let them know you're available to mend some of their finds. Ballroom dancers often need stitchers: sometimes to remake a second-hand costume so it doesn't look familiar to the audience, sometimes to repair the hard use the costumes have taken. Dance costumes can go for $5,000 and up brand new, so many people buy them used and might love to find you.

Self-publish

1) Booklets for tourist stops

Yes, I paid $15 for a pamphlet called "Highlights of the Louvre in 90 minutes or less." (It included instructions like "get off subway here…" "go in this entrance," and other very helpful things, including where the nearest bathrooms and coffee were.)

2) Your own (or other people's) books

Getting published is a whole new ball game these days. The major publishing houses are conglomerates that seem to be in the business of blockbusters, just like the big film studios. With huge advances to earn back, they judge incoming manuscripts solely on how much money they can bring in. If you have your own national TV or radio show or you're a household name for some other reason, they'll be happy to talk to you. If not, you can still try to get their attention, but don't take it personally if you're ignored.

The biggest problem with this kind of publishing has been that quality books that have a small, but often very eager audience might simply disappear. But no more. Self-publishing has taken on a new face with the Print-on-Demand process. Do a search on the internet for 'self publishing' and take a look at the offerings of companies like *iUniverse* and *xLibris.*

3) e-Books

I've already talked about this type of e-book, but it's such a great idea it bears repeating. The hardware required to carry "real" e-Books around with you hasn't become wide-spread yet, so I wouldn't worry about trying to use fancy technology. In fact, you can type up your book in Microsoft Word and when it's just right, hit a button that saves it into something called "PDF" by a company called Acrobat, and presto! Your book will look like a real book right on the screen! (With a table of contents that links to the chapters, to boot.) Then you can give your book a URL location (a site with an address that usually starts with "www."), send out emails to interested parties, and let them read it for free. Or you can send a "teaser" that will make them want to read it, and charge them online for the privilege of getting that URL. (See "N" for Newsletter.)

No books to wrap and ship. Nice and easy—after writing the book, that is.

Support groups

If you'd like to help people who share your interests and/or problems (or you just relate well), how about organizing and running support groups? Support groups are needed for all kinds of people, such as artists, solo business owners, parents of small children, freelance writers, inventors. Contact any group you're already in touch with and offer to create a support group where people can discuss their concerns and get some help from each other. The groups can meet once every month in person to talk, and perhaps more often in a private chatroom or a dedicated bulletin board on a site you'd set up. They could meet periodically, perhaps in a restaurant or after hours in a schoolroom or boardroom to hear experts on any subject they asked you for. You could create and monitor a listserv for them as well. Think how nice that could be if you were working solo in your own business or in a field where you knew no one. You could toss out a question in the middle of the night and get a bunch of answers in your email inbox by morning.

You might want to call your groups "clubs" (such as The NY Artists Club) and charge for membership, but you'd have to offer a very inexpensive fee for starters: you want to draw in enough members to make belonging worth everyone's while. You could also offer individual telephone coaching (see "C" for Coaching). If you develop a reputation for being very helpful, you'll soon have a waiting list for telephone consultations. And every good solution you come up with could be written up into a good email to send to the whole list. Once you have an association you can start offering services by searching for group health insurance, group buying power, etc.

School, start your own

In the July 2003 issue of *Inc. Magazine* there's an article about someone who started a business school in his home. ("The Little Green Schoolhouse" by Ellie Winninghoff.) Gifford Pinchot didn't like what business schools were teaching, so he started his own. It's called the Bainbridge Island Graduate Institute near Seattle, where students study environmental sustainability and social responsibility in the context of entrepreneurship and innovations. It took him only six months to get up and running because instead of spending time and money on a facility, he apparently focused solely on state certification and bringing in a top-notch faculty. The photo in the article shows him sitting on the rug of what looks like a cozy living room with his students. I have a phone call in to him to find out if he's teaching in someone else's home. If he is, his costs are probably rock-bottom.

Sell what you make or do

You don't have to be a door to door encyclopedia salesman to make money selling, and you don't have to think of selling as sleazy or coercive, either. In fact, unless you inherited a huge amount of money from a stranger, you have been selling yourself—your goodness, your smartness, your abilities or something else—to parents, teachers, friends, athletic coaches, casting directors or employers all your life.

You can sell things you make with your hands, things you already own, things you get from others, and of course, you can sell things you do. And you can sell these things in interesting and unusual ways. What are you good at? It doesn't have to be your passion or your life dream, just something you find yourself doing rather well. Now take whatever that is and make it into something sellable. I know a frustrated actor who's only good at two things (besides acting): playing guitar and making balloon animals for his nephews. It took him a while to figure it out, but now he makes most of his living performing at kids' parties: yes, playing guitar and making balloon animals.

Have you been told your banana muffins are the best this side of the Mississippi? Can you knit? Make patterns for stuffed animals? Do makeup or paint faces at parties? Now think of all the places you might sell what you're good at. How about at street fairs, home sales parties, craft shows, at basketball games or picnics in the park, to artists or bankers or plumbers or the small shops in your neighborhood.

If you like to bake cakes, for instance, consider creating novelty cakes that celebrate any old thing and show them to local bakers: baseball cakes for Little Leaguers or a grownup who is a baseball nut. (Ditto with any sport of course. I'd love to see a basketball cake! Or a swimming cake!) If the bakers won't talk to you, put a cake in the optometrist's or shoe-repair shop's window to celebrate the 5th year anniversary of their store. It can help bring in business and if you make the cake big enough, the owner can offer a piece with coffee or milk!

Try answering these questions just for the brain exercise and see how many things you can come up with.

WHAT CAN YOU MAKE OR DO?

- home movies, from camera to DVD
- Victorian goodies
- great cookies
- woven rugs
- sculptured pieces
- perfectly trained dogs
- sound recordings
- photos
- portraits
- etc…

WHERE CAN YOU SELL IT?

- to parents of graduating grade school students
- to restaurants
- on the internet
- at crafts fairs
- at toll booths
- on ferry boats
- outside tourist bureaus
- on Craigslist
- from a pushcart
- from a van

Here's what I thought of when I made my list:

1) Set up a table with computer and a camera with good lights at an antique trade show or swap meet and put people's items on the internet. You can write up the description, manage the sale and keep 25%. They'll feel more secure and you'll have a lot less work to do if you have them keep the item so they can mail it to the buyer. You can also offer them online or telephone classes for learning how to do it all themselves.

2) If you're a cheap clothes junkie and you know where to get the cheapest, best clothes in town but your closet is full, how about finding an old fashioned open truck that goes up and down the streets in the suburbs like they used to do 100 years ago, or like the ice cream man does now, and offering your clothes for sale by calling out on your loudspeaker? You can do this with children's toys, video and computer games or giveaway pets from the ASPCA! You can even play music on the loudspeaker like the ice cream man does!

Storytelling

Some people are enchanting story tellers. It's a gift. They often ask me how they can earn their living as storytellers and some decent ideas have surfaced at some of my Idea Parties:

1) **Perform at school assemblies.** Schools have a budget for hiring educational acts to perform for the student body.

2) **Present at corporate events.** More and more, corporations are seeing what teachers and grandparents have long known: that storytelling can be the best way to teach anything. To find out more about corporate events in an area that interests you take a look at www.go-events.com. It's actually a search engine for nothing but events in fields like Apparel, Building and Construction, Environment and Lifestyle/Entertainment (which includes Wedding and Bridal!) Contact any interesting organization and see what they need. Tell them you can adapt their material to a storytelling form and ask if they'd like you to present at their next conference. (Corporations are cautious. It wouldn't hurt to have a five-minute video of yourself in performance.)

3) **Teach parents how to become better storytellers.** Everyone now knows how important stories are to building a child's imagination. But many parents feel they don't have the ability to make up good stories. Share your talent with others by teaching, either through a website with storytelling techniques and examples (that would be a perfect way to sell your stories if you're a writer), or through classes and/or lectures, which could be the basis for your own book or tape series.

T

Telephone consultations

I love working with people on the telephone and after trying it, clients love phone sessions too. There are unexpected benefits: I have more time to write and even local clients have an easier time scheduling a session if they can arrange for a 3 o'clock phone appointment with me.

If you can offer a service that doesn't require your physical presence, consider setting up phone consultations. You can either set them up via email or do your first consultation in person and later ones on the phone. Be sure to let people know you're available to do sessions on the telephone. Many people prefer it.

Teleclasses

Teleclasses are getting to be big business. Most coaches do the lion's share of their work with clients on the telephone. Teleclass technology gives me an opportunity to set up conference-call meetings with people from all over the world at the same time. Because no travel is required and I can schedule the meeting in the evening, I can do lots of exciting and productive work that my schedule wouldn't allow otherwise. And an added benefit is that the sessions can easily be recorded and made available to others.

I hold three kinds of meetings on the telephone: I work with individuals to help them find and achieve their dreams as usual, but in a teleclass there's an audience. Listeners—who are either hoping to find solutions to their own obstacles or are coaches who want to study my methods and improve their own techniques—can contribute ideas or information during the session and ask questions when the session is completed. I also have Idea Parties on the telephone, with as many as 100 people listening in. The first ten people to register tell their wishes and obstacles and all of us try to come up with solutions to help them. With a group that large, we usually find out exactly what each person needs to know. If you sign up for the next Idea Party, you move up in the line. Finally, I teach real classes on the telephone, on different topics like "Resistance," "Scanners," (a Scanner is a person who wants to do many things and can't settle on one) or how to create a career like mine as a writer and public speaker. I also do training courses for coaches and Success Team leaders using the teleclass technology.

You can do the same with your teaching or consulting. I rent my own telephone line (it's called a "Bridge Line") rather inexpensively. You can find many such opportunities on the internet. It's possible to create a business that takes place entirely on the telephone.

Most people who do this choose to combine telephone work with their computer, and you should consider this as well. You can have a simple, automated system that allows you to

- send out emails announcing your class
- let people pay on the computer so the money goes directly into your bank account

- send them an automated response telling them where to call, and
- send an online receipt with all the information they need.

These systems can cut your administrative work to almost nothing (and, if you're like me, administration is the only part of a teleclass that's not fun.)

There are websites that list telephone classes by dozens of people and even offer teleclasses on how to run teleclasses! Take a look at www.teleclass.com to get a general idea, then do a search on the internet. You'll be amazed at the variety you'll find.

p.s. There are email classes, too (go to "O" for Online Classes).

Travel

If you love faraway places but don't have money for travel, think about these great ideas:

1) Fly for free

Get a credit card that gives you frequent flyer points for every purchase (including additional ones if you actually buy a plane ticket) and use it to pay for *everything*. Just be sure to pay it off before the end of every month. I met a woman who paid her taxes and her kid's tuition (even her rent) on credit cards and traveled all over the world for free. It works. I often fly on business and get frequent flyer points for each flight (plus the points the credit card gives me for buying the ticket in the first place), and I love racking up those miles! I just returned from a round trip to Greece and one to Turkey, and gave a relative a free trip to Indonesia—and I still have miles left! (Take a look at *www.flyertalk.com*

to find out about different programs offered by the airlines. It calls itself "The world's most popular frequent flyer community.")

2) Pick up and go

I recently read an interesting book, *Tales of a Female Nomad: Living at Large in the World*, and I recommend it to people to would love to travel the world but can't imagine how they could possibly do it.

The author, Rita Golden Gelman, describes herself as an affluent (even spoiled) person when she first hit the road. She illustrates brilliantly how someone from a protected life can travel with a backpack and very little money and discover how safe, interesting and enjoyable the world can be. In her words, "I've been living and loving my nomadic existence since the day in 1986 when, at the age of forty-eight, on the verge of a divorce, I looked around and thought, 'There has to be more than one way to do life.'" Read her book and you'll never again say you wish you could travel but you don't have enough money. She has a website you should check out: *www.ritagoldenenglelman.com*).

3) Join the Peace Corps

I've heard very good reports about a book by someone who did, and the reviews alone were enough to make me order it. It's called *Living Poor: An American's Encounter with Ecuador*, by Noritz Thomsen. (You can get it from Eland publishers at *www.travelbooks.co.uk* or do a search for used books on the internet if they no longer print it.) When he was almost 50 the author sold his farm in California and joined the Peace Corps. For four years he lived in a poor village in Ecuador and wrote this book about his experiences. The book got rave reviews from the New York Times Book Review and these words from the San Francisco Chronicle: "This is one of the best kinds of writing and one of the most difficult; the writing that disappears as you read, leaving you with a feeling that you are listening to a man talk; even more important, that you are listening to a man telling the truth."

You don't have to join the Peace Corps and commit to a long stay, however. There are many overseas opportunities that may appeal to you. Search the internet for overseas volunteer opportunities. I found a fascinating site called Charity Focus. Take a look at *http://my.charityfocus.org/my/login/*.

4) Travel as a Courier

Go to *www.travconnect.com* and read (for free) the first chapter of book by David Tinney, President of Adventure Travel Service, Inc. He says, "[I've had] 43 *free* international airline tickets in the last four years. All I've paid is the taxes, less than $63 dollars to Europe." This site came up under the 'courier' search but may have several other strategies including "…turning expenses into free travel." He claims you don't have to own a travel agency to do this. The book is called *Why Not Fly Free?*

www.sinacity.com features a book, "Fly Free, Stay Cheap!: 'How-To' Strategies and Tips for Free Flights & Cheap Travel" by Vicki Mills; Platypus Publications, Inc., June, 1998 ($9.95).

www.flyingsecrets.com features "Fly for Free, with Online Version of our Air Courier Booklet."

DISCLAIMER: All of the above sites are random selections from the first page of a Google search for the terms 'courier + fly free' and I can't vouch for the material offered. But it's a good place to start looking for ideas.

Trade magazines

If you've been trying to find something you'd really love to do, write a list of everything that has ever remotely interested you—even if you're certain it doesn't earn money of any kind, ever. I can almost guarantee there's a magazine devoted to that activity, full of articles by professionals in the field (who are getting paid for what they do). Check them out. Your local library might have them or will be able to find them for you on the internet by entering the name (puppeteers, cartoonists, Mompreneurs). There are worlds out there you don't know about and you could stumble on something that makes your heart beat faster and discover some passion that has eluded you.

When you know what you love, trade magazines are the best way to get an insider's look at the industry as a whole. People who are connected to organizations get important benefits. How do you get connected? Check those trade magazines to find out when and where the next conference, trade show or expo will be and be there. Just sign up and walk in. Listen for awhile until you're ready to ask some intelligent questions and then start talking to people. It could change your life. If you're not good about talking to strangers or you're afraid of feeling like an intruder, drag a friend along.

Theatrical Manager

Almost every actor I speak to says the hardest part of what they do is getting good management. That always gets me thinking about the possibilities. Here are three solutions:

1) if you're an actor who can't get a manager, train one; or

2) if you want to be a manager and turn a good actor into a successful one, find someone you think is talented and ask what he or she would need in a perfect manager. Actors know a lot about what's required and they often know the names and telephone numbers of agents, casting directors and theater owners a manager might need to contact. Your actor can train you to be a great manager; or

3) do both, because they help each other enormously. Continue with your acting career and add a management career as well. I know a very creative actor who was so good at figuring out the ropes (like finding publicity opportunities, using well-placed press releases to fill the seats in theaters, managing introductions with casting directors and discovering parties where the best networking went on) he ended up finding as many opportunities for himself as for his client, and gained great objectivity for what actors should do in the presence of people who were important to their careers (such as agents and casting directors.)

Incidentally, you can manage a band, a model, an artist or photographer or just about anybody. You can also manage a small business and make it successful, like the fairy-godparent every small business owner dreams of. You just have to figure out where your talents and interests lie, and how many clients you can handle; then you'll have an idea of what to charge for your services.

U

Usher

If your secret fantasy is to do nothing but go to theater or concerts, there is a way you can do what you love without starving to death. You can probably find a job (at least a part-time or temporary one) as an usher at live performances. It's an interesting world and you might love it. I'm sure there's a waiting list to usher at major opera houses and theaters, but you can get your start at any performance hall. With that on your resume, you can make yourself available to even the classiest performance halls if you're ready to jump in at the last minute when someone doesn't show. You can easily work your way up from there if you're efficient and agreeable.

When I was in high school I was an usher (we called them usherettes at the time) at the Beverly Canon Theater in Beverly Hills. I saw lots of movie stars who came to see art movies, and I got to dress up in a kimono with long sleeves and a pillow behind my waist. Every night for six months I saw and heard dozens of ten-second fragments of the Kurosawa film "Rashoman". Each time I'd guide latecomers to their seats with my flashlight, I'd hear a few moments of the music, different voices snarling or pleading or chanting, and catch a glimpse of the screen—but never long enough to read the titles, so I had no idea what was being said. But being an usher made me feel like a part owner of the film—a real insider—and it opened up a whole new world to me. Anyway, all my friends were there and we had a very good time being ushers. (And I've heard that director Quentin Tarantino got his start as a clerk in a video rental store, so you never know…)

Events for the Unattached and Unmarried

Someone could start a first-rate business creating interesting, low-stress events for unattached people. Many singles I meet really have a rough go of it. It's hard enough to make the time to socialize and when they do they often find the typical singles scene either boring or downright degrading. Come up with something interesting for singles and you'll be busy, earning money and doing good in this world. To keep costs low (so you can charge enough for your services to make some money), try a potluck dinner and a home-made film festival of great date movies from the past. If you come up with truly jolly ideas for events, and then get a decent mailing list and write decent copy to promote yourself, you will be very successful.

Cocktail parties and single's mixers are excruciating for some of the best single people in the world. How about a "work party" that goes out in the spring to beautify the local parks? I once heard of an organization that once a year selected a privately owned, run-down house and on a certain day in July had all its members show up with any tools or building supplies they had (they got good contractors to join in, and donations from places like Home Depot, as well). On that one day they'd descend on this house (the owner had been warned, of course) and up to 200 people would begin to repair the roof, fix the plumbing and fixtures, as well as the yard and any picket fences in sight. Some people who considered themselves unhandy set up a picnic table and brought food and beverages for all concerned. Others drove vans and pickup trucks back and forth during the day. Within 24 hours, the interior and exterior had been repaired, painted and looked wonderful. (I bet they sometimes came back a second day!)

Now imagine if everyone involved was single. That's a great way to meet people, and to see what they're really like. You're not looking for the "fine-dining and candles" set, though you can throw one of those events from time to time as well.

Create an online center with the best novels, movies (why not throw a weekend film festival?), a list of restaurants that deliver, a video on how to dance the forbidden dance, tips for decor or places to buy romantic sheets. (See also "L" for Love consultant and "F" for Fix someone's life, starting with their apartment.)

Start an Uncles Association

Is there such an organization? No. But there should be, so why don't you start one? If your brother or sister has a baby you have a splendid opportunity to become a true Uncle. To fulfill the delicious stereotype of being an aunt, a woman needs to be colorful, even wacky, and intervene on her niece's or nephew's behalf when their parents are being...well, parents. Uncles, on the other hand must travel to foreign lands and bring back amazing and hair-raising tales (preferably about their personal involvement with alligators or small airplanes), as well as exotic objects like fake shrunken heads or shark's teeth. They must also be able to teach their nieces and nephews some exotic art, like 12-string guitar, chess or ululation. (Ul-u-late: verb, to howl or wail in grief or jubilation). If your sibling's kids live in the city, yodeling might be good enough to impress them.

The special needs and training for first-time uncles hasn't (to the best of my knowledge) ever been undertaken. Who tells uncles what size clothes to buy a baby or youngster, what's considered hip among the nine-year old set, where one can get an electronic drum set with headphones for under $1,000...stuff like that? It could be an industry, with a website, newsletter, bulletin board, Frequently Asked Questions and an affiliate program if you send viewers to sites where they can shop for books (and trips to the Antarctic!)

Somebody ought to do it. It's needed and it's fun: you can create a special Uncle's Catalog of books and CDs, video cameras, ant farms and Go Fish! card games to send to your whole mailing list. It's surely an idea whose time has come.

Used Book Dealer

Sell used and rare books on the internet

Until recently, used book dealer always sold their books in stores or at book fairs, or mailed out printed catalogues of what they had in stock, but one day I found a dealer in travel literature who sold his books from his apartment.

"They're not all here," he said when I visited him. "I have a warehouse in New Jersey, too. I once had a store but the rents got too high so I was limited to book fairs."

"And now you sell books from here?" I asked, assuming all his customers came to his home as I was doing.

"No, I sell them from there," and he pointed into another room where, on a nearly-empty round table with a lace tablecloth sat a laptop computer.

206

"Really?" I said. "You can sell enough books on the internet to keep you going?"

"They paid for this apartment," he said. Considering real estate prices in the neighborhood, I was impressed with that statement.

Selling books on the internet is old hat now, but he's still doing fine online and I can appreciate why. Though I love spending time in dusty, old bookstores and have searched through them in every town I've visited, it was unusual to find what I wanted. I remember the hours spent in vain looking for certain books, knowing in my heart that the books I wanted were sitting in some bookstore in a city I'd never visit. Bringing the buyer to the seller is a tough problem in this business. Or was. Once I got on the mailing list of a website connected with my interest (it's geography and history of mountainous regions if you're getting curious), I found the books I needed in bookstores in Australia, South Africa, and South Carolina, too.

Used Anything Dealer

I won't go into this one in detail but you do know that if you've got the time and the patience you can go to swap meets and junkyards—or drive around your town the night everyone puts out the big stuff for the trash pickup—find things, fix them up, and sell them at flea markets, swap meets, antique-ish stores, and on eBay. It's a lot of work, but if you enjoy it, you won't mind; I know retired and unemployed couples who do well because they share the work.

Now think about some unusual ways of selling used things in person: You can travel to flea markets around the country, sure (nothing new there) but what if you had a traveling flea market? I never heard of one of these. You could create a Caravan of many vehicles and carry your flea market anywhere. Advertise in the local papers and show up on the given date. Set up in open lots or schools or even parking garages that empty out on the weekends (like New York's weekend 6th Avenue flea markets on 26th street).

The key is either to go where there are no organized flea markets or to bring things that aren't easy to find locally. In big cities you can bring flea markets full of kitsch from the hinterlands. (Also handmade items, old typewriters and peculiar-looking furniture might go over big.) To small towns you might bring lightly used electronics or health foods—well, not *used* health foods, but you get my point—or whatever is uncommon in rural areas.

V

Victorian items and Victorian settings

These are very appealing to many people. I regularly receive a catalog of Victorian goodies to buy—some of which are a little vampiry and Gothic novel-ish, many which are simply loveable and for which I am a total sucker—like dolls and water pitchers. Here are some jolly ideas that might wake up that total sucker in you—and, more to the point, wake it up in other people who are willing to buy from you. You can create gifts or household articles, give Victorian garden parties, take people on tours of Victorian homes, have a monthly program of Victorian films or TV series. (Some of these things you can do for special groups, like corporations or singles or seniors.)

Have a Victorian weekend in the country

Have you heard of those murder mystery events that are held (often for corporations) as entertainment for groups of people? Take that form, remove the murder and add a Victorian tale. Find a beautiful old home available for renting or a bed and breakfast (preferably one with a veranda and somewhere to stroll) and create a program. You'll need some actors to play cameo appearances of brothers back from India, doctors who stay for dinner and hold forth on literary matters, a resident aged matriarch with an iron will. You can provide light costumes, such as shawls and hats for the ladies, jackets with boutonnieres for the gentlemen. While there will be breaks in which people can be themselves, you should have hour-long sessions (at meals, on some walks) in which there is a story line—of the type where improvisation is possible. There will be generalized roles for each person to draw out of a hat (the jealous one, the brilliantly successful one, the shy genius, the eager swain, the cynic who wishes to marry for money, the old family friend who knows there is no money, etc.)

And (Oh, I do love this one) you can do it on a train instead of at a house! My mom contributed that idea, because she remembers people doing exactly that in the 1930's. (And what's wrong with a Ferry boat? Or a side-wheeling giant paddle Mississippi River Boat! Bring the video cameras.) Regardless of location, in the evening people can relax, watch a Merchant-Ivory film or an episode of "Upstairs, Downstairs" or sit by the fire and play cards, drink sherry and talk among themselves, maybe even have a small dance.

You can publicize this idea cheaply by going on local radio and TV, and/or you can get a sponsor—or more than one—who'd like the opportunity to advertise their product and be seen as a good guy. You need a website and a mailing list if you really want to get good momentum going, but you can probably start out with flyers posted to bulletin boards around town. (Wouldn't this make a great fundraising benefit? Offer it—at a fair price—to philanthropies.)

Selling Victorian Crafts

Lots of people produce crafts, but finding a way to sell them is often a problem. You can sell through a catalog or try to get department stores to carry your work, but that means you must produce hundreds of each kind of item. For most craftspeople, this is no fun at all. Like painters and sculptors, each piece they work on is meant to be one of a kind. Wouldn't it be wonderful to open your own showroom, have people come to you (without spending any money on advertising) and keep the full price of anything you sell? For most craftspeople this means being limited to crafts fairs or selling their work on the internet. But I just read about a group of women who came up with an inspired solution that avoids both of those methods.

A number of years ago, two women were looking for work they could do at home because they had disabled children. They began creating Victorian items to sell. They bought pieces at thrift stores and re-fashioned them into one-of-a-kind items, crocheted pretty doilies and tea cozies, made shawls and lampshades, and found and matched up vintage china tea sets. One of them started doing Victorian tea parties for her friends using these items, and soon the invited friends were purchasing them.

After a while, a few other talented women joined these two and together they were so prolific they soon had hundreds of beautiful items and nowhere to sell them. They didn't have the money to rent a boutique, and with children who had special needs, they couldn't sit in a store all day in any event. What they needed, they decided, was a big private show four times a year. But, where?

Their solution was ingenious. Four times a year, one of the members (with the help of all the others) moves almost everything in her home into the garage and her home becomes the showroom for that season. What goes into the nearly empty house? Every corner of every room is filled with tapestries, hand-painted tables, dried flower arrangements, lamps made from beautiful pitchers, lace-edged fans, groups of small, festooned and beribboned lampshades for chandeliers, statuary and refurbished porcelain dolls with new costumes, restored doll houses, decorated straw hats and cleaned and mended vintage clothing, tapestry covered footstools, lace antimacassars, fringed window shades with tasseled pulls, clocks and mirrors, odd little repainted tables and every other item the women have been working on in their homes for the previous three months.

They dress up quite grandly for the occasion—wearing long dresses and fine hats—and serve tea in the garden with a photographer in attendance for customers who want photos to take home. They have hundreds of fans, some who plan their vacations around the dates of these home shows. They've been doing this for almost 15 years and have a mailing list of over 3,000 people. For photos and info, visit their charming site at *www.grandvictorianboutique.com.*

Van-based businesses

If you have a van or can get one, there are a lot of business opportunities out there. You can offer delivery services in your neighborhood, open a bookmobile for kids or romance novel fans, or set up a mobile computer lab. In fact, you can take almost any idea in this book at put it "on wheels". I'll bet you can come up with many more ideas based on where you live and what skills or resources you have. Here are some ideas to stimulate your creativity.

Pet Taxi Service

If you're not interested in walking the dog, then maybe you might take him for a ride! Is there anyone in your town who does this? If not—and you really like animals—this might be a great job for you. You'd be taking the cat to the vet, picking her up and bringing her home. With so many families away for the day, this is a well-needed service. Think of the elderly, who can't take their pets to get their shots or checkups. You'll need a setup to safely transport the animal—a large space or cage in your van, a place to hook up the leash so your charges don't suddenly jump out when the doors are open, that sort of thing. Carry some promotional materials to leave in veterinary offices, pet stores and the dog park.

Mobile Gallery

Under "S" (Sell what you make or do) I suggested using a van as a means for selling things you create (like portraits, for example). This idea deserves more attention, I think. It can be so difficult to get people to see and buy your work, although the internet and open markets are a huge step forward from the traditional store-based method and all of its heartache. But these also require getting people to come and that's not always easy. Why not take the work to them? In general, people are fairly passive consumers but if you have an unusual venue you can often grab their attention long enough to notice your work.

If you pulled up to a corner on a warm day, to a spot where people were walking around, and opened the door of your van to reveal your unique sculptures or hand made jewelry, you'd surely draw a crowd. (You might have some trouble with the authorities if you were selling beer, or Levis in front of a Gap store, but they are much more lenient if it's your material.)

Of course, this is also a perfect way to publicize your work: get a paper to do a story on your unorthodox style of art and selling...or hand out a flyer with your philosophy and direct people to your website.

Volunteer

You've heard it before: volunteering is a great way to learn something new, and make contacts with people who can help you with your dream. It's true: even if your dream is just to meet wonderful people, volunteering will still give you a classy resume you might need some time in the future—and it will make you feel like a million bucks because you're a good guy and you're doing something that makes a difference to people. You could change some lives, and that's nothing to sneeze at.

IMPORTANT TIP: If you just don't know where to start looking for a volunteer opportunity that will suit your talents and gifts and make you happy, head over to *www.goodthings.com*. You must never volunteer for anything that doesn't meet those criteria unless it's an emergency, because you'll be unhappy, resentful and guilty—and you'll do a lousy job; you'll be hurting yourself and, worst of all, you might give up on volunteering altogether, thinking (incorrectly) that it isn't any fun.

You can get a start right now by checking out these useful sites:

www.volunteermatch.com

www.volunteer.org (for international opportunities)

www.worldvolunteerweb.org (UN portal to resources, information, news and global networks)

www.interaction.com

www.idealist.com

www.careerinsocialchange.com

www.oneworld.net (a comprehensive British site covering organizations all over the world dealing with every kind of problem.

Do Voiceovers

Have you ever gotten compliments on your speaking voice and wished you could use that voice to earn some money? Then you've probably considered getting into voiceovers. A voiceover is the voice you hear on radio and TV commercials, or the voice you hear talking while you're watching a documentary on television, explaining that the cheetah is about to chase a wildebeest. If you don't know anything about voiceovers but you've fantasized being the voice of a cartoon character on TV (or the subject interests you in some way), I'm happy to be able to share this with you: there's actually an incredibly helpful website dedicated specifically to that, not run by a big commercial company but a person who does voiceovers herself. The site is: *www.avoiceabovethecrowd.com*. Among many other goodies, she has an "Advice and Links" page that can get you started, and you'll find a list of books that will show you anything you need to know.

Her name is Karen Commins, and she says: "I do want to gently point out that voice-over is not something that you can just 'take a stab at.' Like any dream, it takes tremendous commitment and persistence...I created my advice page on my website because so many people have written to me saying 'I have a nice voice; how do I do voice-over?'"

(Incidentally, Karen's site is an excellent example of how one can offer valuable, free information while bringing in income from affiliate programs, book sales and services.)

WHERE SHOULD YOU START?

Ad agencies are looking for you because they make commercials. Television production houses might want your services as well. The bigger markets like New York are hard to break into but at a workshop I recently held in Des Moines a man who stood up and said (in an amazing, deep voice) that his dream was to do voices was absolutely rushed by three people in the business who wanted his card, and the producer from IPTV, the public television station that was filming the workshop, said he'd have gone up too because they always need voices like that, but he thought he'd give the other people a chance.

So, while it's not as easy as just creating a demo tape and sending it off to ad agencies, marketing gurus and casting directors and then waiting for the offers to roll in, don't let anyone tell you this is a "pie-in-the-sky" career. Look at the ideas given by Karen and others on my bulletin board and see what you think. (There are even some good suggestions for people who live in New York!)

- Read the theater news magazine, "Backstage". (You can find it in most big bookstores or on the net at *www.backstage.com*.)

- Here's another site to visit: *www.voice-overs.com*.

- Do a search on the internet for "voiceovers" and you'll see examples of sites by people looking for voiceover work, companies who want to train you to do voiceovers, voice coaches, articles from "Variety" (you can get a free trial subscription to see if it's useful), and even a site that offers a tutorial for recording a voiceover in an Adobe program.

- If you're in a city with adult education programs, take some classes. You'll not only learn the ropes, you'll probably find that your teacher is in the business and might even be looking for good talent to represent. To find adult ed classes in your city, check out ads in your newspaper or the yellow pages or contact the Chamber of Commerce.

- Talk to performing artists and musicians or teachers in acting schools. They're in the same business.

These suggestions are especially brilliant:

- Volunteer to do voiceovers for your public television station and get your voice out there. It will look great on your resume. Also, voices are needed in small towns for cable advertising on the local stations. They might let you have a copy for your demo tape if you do volunteer work for them.

- If you live in a small town, contact an advertising account executive at any radio, TV, or cable system in your area and tell them you'd like to voice one of their ads if they ever happen to need a different voice. As a TV producer in a small market said, "I'd love to have someone fill in for me so it isn't my voice on every other commercial that comes on!"

spinoff idea: **Help others do voiceovers**

One of the biggest obstacles for most of us is that we just hate selling ourselves. On the other hand, we don't mind selling someone else, especially if we believe in their ability. That means that you can start a buddy system, or even a small Success Team dedicated to people who need someone to agent and manage them for voiceover work and do it for each other! You'll have plenty of courage and imagination for everyone else, and they will for you, too. You might even include someone in the team who also has a sound studio and skills in sound engineering or recording (or has people in his or her family who do), who can help all of you make your own demos. Think of it: a group of five or six people, finding the ad agencies and casting directors and promoting each other until every single one of you becomes successful. If you do that, please call me because I'm going to put you in my next book!

W

Website, yours

Do you have any idea how many incredible things you can do with your own website? If you've been wondering why you'd want one, go back to the beginning of this book and circle all the paragraphs with the word "website" in them and read them again. You'll begin to see the huge range of valuable services a site can offer you.

Yes, you should have one. You can start with a free website, just to get a sense of what they are from the inside. Go to any search engine like Yahoo and they'll help you put it up. Yahoo's web hosting site is called "GeoCities" (*www.geocities.com*) and there you can create *your own free website today*. Those free sites are not meant for commercial purposes, and they're not what you'd want to do business on, anyway. (GeoCities also offers full-powered, professional sites which they'll set up and maintain for a small monthly fee. Check it out.) After a while, you'll know something about how a website can be laid out. Then you can go looking at the websites of other people. You'll understand what you're seeing and be able to appreciate the power available to you: to teach, to be found by customers, to create, to learn—there is no end to the way you can use a website to help you do what you love. And make money at it.

There are so many uses for a website, I won't try to list them all here, but

1) If you're starting a business, or already have one, a website serves as both your business card and your press kit. For so many years I struggled to keep folders and articles and new materials all ready to send out in press kits. My little home office got overwhelmed by having to tailor and package each press kit for each situation, and half the time the recipient would say it had gotten lost so I had to send another. That ended when I got a website. Now, I just tell people to visit my site and we let a lot of trees continue to stand—and have so many fewer headaches than before. Even if you want hard copies of a press kit, and brochures to hand out at meetings or conferences or trade shows, you still need a site for people to go to when they want to know more, or to

contact you without fear of the kind of high-pressure selling they might get from a personal phone call.

2) For any kind of promotion you want to do, your website is a fantastic marketing and sales tool. If you've written a book, for instance, you can display the cover on the home page and let viewers see the table of contents and sample pages. You create an order form so people can send you money online and then you can mail them your book. How will they know you have a website in the first place? You'll write them an email—a short one—with a link to your site. How can you avoid being deleted as "spam" (internet junk mail)? By writing individual emails to each person or by using your own carefully assembled mailing list. (See "M" for Mailing List.)

3) When you want to offer your expertise to the world but you're not ready to go out there and deliver personal presentations (or no one will invite you!), your website will let you feel confident while you practice. One person I know wanted to be a public speaker and had a message that she longed to share with the world, but she had extreme stage-fright and described herself as an introvert. However, she had no problem creating a newsletter/e-zine, full of short articles on her subject, and sending them to people. Her site allowed people to email questions to her, and soon she found she could put up a "Dear Abby" kind of column on her site with the answers she gave them. After a short time, she began to run private chat rooms on Instant Messaging—a live exchange where you type your answers to questions as they come in on the computer screen. Finally, she sent out a mailing (her list was connected to her site so people could easily sign up on their own) announcing that she would run

a live telephone presentation on a Wednesday evening on some topic, with questions and answers at the end. It was such a success she's now eager to talk face to face with people as soon as she can arrange it. But she'll never give up her website. If she starts to give presentations regularly, she'll want a place that lists her upcoming appearances.

4) Websites are fun! I gave my mother one for her 87th birthday (called *www.mymothersdresses.com*) because I loved her stories and drawings of the dresses she had worn through the years. I put her drawings on the site and even an audio of her voice talking about each dress as she drew it: ("Now this was Sarah's blouse… it had beautiful gold stitching right here along the collar and tiny cloth-covered buttons. But if I got up early enough I'd pinch it to go to school. She always forgave me. With five sisters we always said, 'The first one up is the best one dressed!'"). I had a techie add a photo album of her sisters and brothers, and of us kids too, with our kids, and showed it to her on my computer on her birthday. She liked it well enough, thinking it was a sort of slide show and nothing more until my oldest son called her from Italy and said, "Happy birthday, Grandma! You're famous all over the world! My friends in Bologna are looking at your drawings right now!" That impressed her.

I'm barely scratching the surface of what a website of your own can do for you. You just do what I said when we started this topic: go back to the beginning of this book and circle every paragraph with the word "website" in it and you'll see even more fascinating, useful ways a website can be used.

And then there are weblogs. Oh, how easy they are, and what potential they have.

Weblog

What if you don't have or want the skills to put up a website and don't want to pay for someone who does? You can have a totally loveable new kind of website that you'll be able to run all by yourself without knowing a word of computer code. I call it a website "for the rest of us." You can create a weblog— or 'blog' as they're affectionately known–and I promise you'll never look back. A weblog is a site which is essentially an online journal or personal diary, and you'll find lots of them which are exactly that. Some of them might not do much for you ("Here is Skootchy with her new catnip mouse. You can't exactly see her in this picture but she is so funny!")

Are they hard to do? Well, someone has to show you how to get started, but then it's a lot easier than driving a stick-shift car or touch-typing. For an example of how easy it is, take a look at gorgeous kilims as they're woven every day in a little Turkish village on a very simple weblog which you can find at *www.kilimwomen.com.* This site is done entirely by the girls in the program and last year they didn't know how to push the 'On' button of a computer!

I had the best time following one blog of the journey of four young women across the Taklamakan Desert in China, with their weekly photos and entries. (I still can't figure out how they sent their entries in from the back of a camel!)

And be sure to take the time to go back to "J" for Journal Keeper in this book to re-read the section on creating weblogs for homebound or elderly people who want to tell their stories—who they were on this earth, what they did and thought, and what happened to them. I think you'll be inspired.

Be a Writer

Don't assume you have to take up heavy smoking (and drinking), go live in a cabin in the woods or a shack by the beach and open a vein every time you write, only to find you probably don't have a chance of getting published, much less making any money. Do you have any idea how many jobs there are for writers?

Look around you: everything has writing on it. Someone was hired to do that writing and a whole lot of people make a living at it. Writers are hired for ad copy, magazine articles, brochures, resumes, business proposals, and the list goes on and on. The internet boom made the writer invaluable, with web pages needing to be updated daily and all the e-zines that require writers to do research and create articles. It's a great time to be a freelance writer.

Know your market.

Check out *www.freelancewriting.com* to get a sense of who needs what you want to do. Writing is needed (and paid for) in places you'd never think of. Corporations need employees to be able to create clear reports and memos. City and state governments, hospitals and medical schools—any organizations you can think of—need writers for their newsletters, grant proposals, correspondence, brochures, information booklets and quarterly reports. Every ad agency would love to have talented, reliable freelance writers waiting for overflow work.

Actually, almost every business or organization mentioned here needs people who *teach* writing just as much as they need actual writers. And companies with foreign born employees are in great need of someone to help teach English skills. A writer can usually get a job like that without any teaching credentials if he or she is already teaching writing in the company. From all accounts by people who have taught such classes, they are extremely enjoyable and gratifying: the students are very eager to learn and highly appreciative of their teachers.

If you know how to write, consider being a writing coach. If you're experienced you can meet your writer clients on the phone, through the internet or in person if you like, and help keep them moving ahead with their writing projects. But you can have a bigger hand than that in the writing. Becoming a memoir coach (yes, that's a real thing and someone is doing it: see "C" for Coaching) allows you to help older people get their words on paper, many of whom really do want to leave their stories for grandchildren to read one day.

There's probably a great book in describing your experiences helping seniors write their stories. For sure, they could fill a great website and/or weblog which could entertain and inspire many people and bring in more gigs for you at the same time. To get publicity you can interest journalists in what you're doing and get articles written about you. For example, you'd send an email to a columnist with this teaser in it: "Bessie talks about how her great-grandmother met her husband while milking a goat under a table in 1908 in a little village in the Ukraine" and when they click on the link, they're on your site where they can read Bessie's story (that you wrote for her). Whoever reads it just might start thinking about how they'd like you to do the same thing for them—or their grandmother. (All the interviews can be done on the telephone, remember, and even recorded for all the great-great grandchildren to hear in years to come.) Of course, now we're getting back into that idea of a weblog autobiography I love so much, and if you use the latest weblog technology you can also have video or create a slide show of early photos from the author, and you can email all the relatives for their comments and contributions from anywhere in the world. God, I love that idea.

Learn how to write

What if you don't feel you write well enough to try out these ideas? Well, you can learn how from the convenience of your own home. If you're not familiar with the specifics of the writing arena you want to enter, you can learn from some excellent teachers right from your computer—online, late at night or at 4 in the morning, from Fargo, North Dakota or Papua, New Guinea. Search the internet for writing teachers, schools and coaches. When I did that I found dozens of them and I also got the chance to continue my enthusiasm for weblogs from a writing teacher at De Anza College (*http://faculty.deanza.fhda.edu/jocalo*) and I was fascinated to read what it's like to be in a writing class from the perspective of the teacher!

There are online writing classes galore, and you don't have to sign up at a college to take them. Gotham Writers' Workshop (*www.writingclasses.com*), for instance, has classes on writing anything from fiction and drama to travel, memoirs, sitcoms and stand-up comedy.

No excuses anymore. If you've got a telephone and a computer—or a library in your town that will let you use a computer—you can polish your writing skills and write for a living.

Earn lots of money with your Writing

You can make a lot of money writing and you don't have to write a blockbuster novel, either.

And just in case you don't read introductions, let me mention Robert W. Bly again. He's either got the secret for writing lots of books fast or he simply has the metabolism of a chipmunk, but he's smart and he's a good writer. His information is thorough and very useful. The book I have in front of me right now is *Secrets of a Freelance Writer: How to Make $85,000 a Year*. Writer's Digest often publishes articles by him, and you should try to find a very good one called "Teach and Grow Rich" written in Feb. of 1997, but still on target. Here's the lead: "With fees ranging from $100 to $4,000 a day, teaching writing often pays better than writing itself. Here are some steps you can take to join the lucrative speaking, consulting, training seminar and workshop business."

Last but not least, a first-rate book, *The Well-Fed Writer: Financial Self-Sufficiency as a Freelance Writer in Six Months or Less*, by Peter Bowerman (Fanove Publishing, Atlanta GA). His dedication, incidentally, is to Bob Bly, "who gave me the idea in the first place. You're my hero." He started his writing career from nowhere, he says, and did very well within six months. You'll understand it when you see how well he writes, but that's not nearly enough to make it, and he'll be the first to tell you. Fortunately, he gives a down-to-earth, step-by-step method for being a successful writer-for-hire. And he doesn't like working long days or long weeks either, so his system is very doable if you want time to pursue other things or have other commitments.

Ghostwriting

Have you ever thought about ghostwriting? I spoke to a ghostwriter who told me something very interesting I want to pass on to you. She attended conferences, listened to speakers and then, if she liked them, went up front afterwards to ask them if they had written a book. If they said no, she offered to do it for them. This was in the late 1990's and prices may have changed, but she said her assistants charged $5,000 to do a book, and she charged $15,000. (If you get involved with a book packager, I promise you'll have lots of work. They find interesting people, put them together with ghostwriters, design the whole book and give the finished project to a publisher, making life very easy for publishers.)

Write fiction

Even with fiction, smoking, drinking and agonizing are no longer required. In fact, it can be a lot of fun if you do it with your friends. I know of a group of women who sat down together and wrote two short murder mysteries set in their own suburb, with housewives and mothers complaining loudly as they tracked down the murderers. They never got a publisher, but they should try again and publish their own books with a brand new kind of publishing company. These days you don't have to buy 5,000 books and keep them in your garage while you try to sell them, because there's a remarkable new technology called "print on demand" or "P.O.D."; and there are publishers who will print a beautiful book for you at a very low cost and let you sell it any way you like. (You probably know by now which that way would be: the internet and your own website.)

Self-publishing has made producing a book so accessible for anyone wanting to make a small investment with a big return. Check out these websites to get an idea if self-publishing is for you:

www.iuniverse.com
www.trafford.com
www.u-publish.com

X

Xmas

Are you a pretty good singer? Do you know how to make nice decorations, or knit cute socks...or bake a decent cake? Those don't seem like big money makers, but every year in December people who wouldn't consider themselves professionals make good money with their talents and hobbies for the holidays— sometimes enough to support themselves for months!

Here are some ideas I've come across:

- Singers in big cities make money at Christmas singing in churches, but many of them stand on the sidewalk to sing their Bach and find some good change in their hats. Or they sing at rich people's parties for even better pay.

- Throw a Christmas ball and make it glamorous enough for people to pay decent money for tickets.

- Be a Christmas coach for a small town and put them on the map by creating and publicizing colorful events that will bring tourists from miles away. If you can interest the Chamber of Commerce in creating a great downtown event to pull everyone away from online catalogs so they'll buy from the local shopkeepers, they'll pay your fee (and it can turn into a yearly event with reliable income for you).

- Set up a Christmas Pageant Wagon to roll through towns, carrying singers and actors for musical or theatrical performances like they did in the Middle Ages. You might be hired to bring it to more than one town during the holiday season and find yourself the owner of an interesting seasonal business.

And here are some spin-offs:

You could get hired as a Christmas Coach (above) and get carolers ready for first-rate performances, to bring cheer to any down-at-the-heels town that's lost a lot of jobs and just sinks further into the blues at Christmas. Maybe you could actually help that same little town get on the map with a cottage industry for decorations made out of something unusual and loveable, like salt dough animals, angels, Santas painted, packaged and ready to ship, or some other amazing Xmas industry! If the objects are interesting enough—or the story of how the town is saving itself has warmth and what the media calls "human interest"—you won't have to compete with big catalogues because you can get them in the newspapers and on TV. (If you've got a PR background, this will be perfect for you. If you don't, find someone who does!)

How about selling vintage children's books that you've gathered from thrift stores through the year…or creating children's books that tell the story of each town and how it has celebrated Christmas since it was founded? If you gather stories and photos from the local townspeople and credit them on the pages, you'll sell out in every town.

Or how about expanding the book idea and opening a real Christmas museum full of photos and items from everyone's attic, showing how small town America celebrated Christmas in the 1800's?

Somebody somewhere makes all those costumes for the Santas who stand in front of department stores ringing bells all over the western world. If your town had a clothing factory it might be interesting to find a way to compete with them. Or how about having a Santa training school? You could train people who want to play Santa, of course. I'm not sure what a paid Santa would need to learn, but how about a Santa School for Dads—and Moms, too. Mrs. Santa needs an outfit of her own and I've never seen one interesting enough to remember. They can leave the kids with Grandma and give themselves the pre-Xmas present of a weekend vacation at Santa School learning how to assemble the presents they bought and how to say "Ho-Ho!" with the proper baritone. Or start a different kind of Xmas industry, like making and renting or selling fabulous hand-decorated sleighs and training a herd of small reindeer to rent out with them. Lots of other Chambers of Commerce might rent them. Maybe schools, or Rotary Clubs too!

Xanadu

Sometimes all you need is a word or a poem or an image in your mind to bring out your best ideas. Take the fantasy idea of the place called Xanadu. That's where the poet Coleridge said Kublai Khan decreed a stately pleasure dome. He didn't get to tell us much more because he was (famously) interrupted by a neighbor and never got around to finishing the poem, but what little he did write was so gorgeous and haunting that it has fascinated people ever since. What could you do with the notion of Xanadu? A symbol this strange and beautiful is bound to be a great source of ideas. (In fact, if you do a search on the internet for "Xanadu" you'll find that it's been used to name businesses, fiction, personal hideaways and software that does data analysis for X-Ray Astronomy. Coleridge would be amazed. It's public domain by now so you can use it too. What could you do with Xanadu?

Here are some ideas to get you started:

1) Run a class or workshop on descriptive writing. (Call it "Gorgeous Writing," if you want to attract some attention.)

2) Offer to bring poetry readings of the Romantic poets to people's Valentine's Day parties.

3) Teach artists how to say no to people who knock on their doors when they're in the middle of working!

4) Take people on a tour of "Kublai Khan's World". He wasn't just your average 13th Century Chinese Emperor, you know. He's the one who hired Marco Polo to work for him and regretfully let him return home to Venice after 14 years of good service (well, according to Marco Polo, anyway.)

Xenophobia therapist

[xen.o.pho.bi.a (zee-no-FO-bee-ya) *(noun): an intense fear or dislike of foreign people, their customs and culture, or foreign things.*]

I have relatives who fear and dislike people who are different from them. While I personally consider these relatives to be much scarier than the people they fear, the fact is that sometimes xenophobic people have to travel or even live in countries where their jobs (or a family member's job) require them to be, and it would be wonderful for everyone if they got over their discomfort and dislikes.

So how on earth do you change this? Well, there are lots of clever ways you can at least get the sharp edges off, and if you're willing to tailor your program to the particular reactions of individuals—in the way people help clients with a phobia about flying in airplanes—you can build a decent reputation and get hired by some corporations with deep pockets and the motivation to give you what you're worth to them.

I wouldn't start with immersion, however. I'd fight fear with lovability. Start with movies, the warmest and funniest movies made about the people in question. I'd have cooking classes for the new kind of food, teach history classes that show the feared people's past in the best light. If you've got U.S. Westerners heading for China, for example, you can awe them with the history of the Heavenly Horses that sweated blood and bankrupted the Emperor of China because he wanted them so much, and you can impress them with films that show the astonishing riding skills of central Asians. You can interest homemakers in the variety of households, and surprise them with the luxury of Mongolian yurts. You can tell tales of heroes and heroines, play the music and show the dances. You can highlight the fashions or the gardens.

Most of all, you have to show the individual people as they really are close-up, and nothing can do that as safely and as well as telling stories and showing documentaries or films. (For instance, who could help loving Hottentot Bushmen after seeing "The Gods Must Be Crazy"?)

Y

Yacht entertainer

People on yachts may love slow, lazy days at sea, but they get bored all the same. If you left some nice flyers down at the Marina, or even held some free outdoor events to draw a crowd and give the audience your flyers, you might get hired as an entertainer of some kind, such as a story teller or even someone who reads a great novel out loud. I bet there are people who wish they had read *The Brothers Karamazov* by Dostoyevsky but know they never will. You could ensconce yourself in one of the rooms or on one side of the deck and read out loud. (If it's a round-the-world trip, take Proust!)

We're talking yachts here, not sailboats, so there's also room for you put on a play using the guests as actors. That can be lots of fun for them. Or, if they'd rather not get involved, you can also bring a cast with you and put on the play— or a whole repertory, before being let off in Barbados and flown home.

Truth be known, there's more of a hunger for intellectual fare out there than you realize, and if you wanted to teach a class about opera or art, you'd probably get some interest. I think the whenever "experts" are invited on cruises they're always in finances, investments, or cryogenics (that means getting yourself frozen and waking up when your stock is worth more or some such thing) or just more fashion/jewelry shows.

People who go on yachts also have children, so entertaining or tutoring kids on yachts could be a great opportunity, too. To be honest, I can't figure out how

I'd look that one up on the internet unless someone somewhere wrote an article about it. You never know. Still, if you're a sea-loving soul, your best bet is to become known in a marina as a reliable person by the shopkeepers and others. And then, to show off where you can be seen!

This is an odd enough profession to interest journalists if you bring it to their attention, and if you get written about be sure to copy that article! It makes you look...legitimate. Then attach it to your flyer. (Get into yachter's trade magazines and you'll get some phone calls for sure!)

Create a Yam festival

Don't laugh: I've heard about towns that throw Garlic festivals and Chili festivals, which attract hundreds (or even thousands) of visitors every year. You could do this in a number of ways:

1) In your town

2) Online for towns in rural areas that actually raise the things, to help them get publicity for their yams

3) As a traveling festival through yam country, or as an addition to state fairs. Have a cooking contest, sell recipes and cookbooks or help them do it—teach kids how to carve yam faces, speak about the fabulous health benefits, the zoo-geography and history of yams through the ages, some fun anthropology (I believe it's New Guinea, where the paranoid cultures thought neighbors sang the yams away into their own gardens).

Yarn

Knit or weave with it. Buy and sell it. Or go far from home to some inhospitable islands, work for sheep farmers until you can get your own spread (which you could call "Haldane Farms") and then start a label of your own (say, "Black Sheep Designs") and do hand-knitting, machine-knitting, design work, hand-spinning, dyeing, crocheting. Write books and make greeting cards, make looms and carve crochet needles.

Yes, it *can* be done, and it has been, in the Falkland Islands. If you want to see a charming site and hear the story of the people who started Black Sheep Designs on their own spread (with about five miles of coastline!) go to *www.falklandwool.com* and treat yourself to a 20-minute vacation.

If you love yarn and spinning and knitting or other fiber arts, you'll find a long list of great links on this site, including some dedicated to sheep shearing. (Also some British Antarctic Surveys and a Penguin Picture Gallery, to say nothing of a local miniature horse farm!)

Z

Okay, granted, you're not going to find that many ideas that begin with "Z", but there are some. Take a look at these ideas and see what else you can come up with. (It's good practice for becoming a real idea person!)

Zoo keeper

How about a zoo astrologer? Or zoo manicurist? Or zoo Philatelist? Or dentist? Beautician? Naw. But how about a zoo psychologist for animals in cages? Betcha $5 there is such a thing!

Zarzuela

Zarzuela: a type of Spanish musical theater, usually comic, combining dialogue, music and dance. Produce it for public schools to help kids understand a new culture.

Zen board game

Create one to help people do the Zen thing: you know, be all there and don't get attached to outcomes and stuff. (I don't know how you'd keep score, though!)

Zombie

Play one at children's parties (not all kids want a loveable clown you know). Sew and sell zombie costumes.

EPILOGUE

Are you becoming an Idea Person? If these pages have helped you start thinking more creatively, I've achieved my goal. I hope you can now see how many ways there are to do what you love (and have fun doing it) without breaking the bank, getting a loan, taking huge risks, going after expensive, time-consuming credentials or making terrible sacrifices.

Even if you felt you had no clue what you want to do, I'm guessing these ideas have helped you rediscover what it is you *love*. How do ideas help you figure out what you love? As I've learned through almost 40 years of working with individual clients, hearing fresh and original ideas, seeing unexpected solutions to the problem of how to do what you love in the real world, these make hidden dreams step out of hiding and loudly announce themselves.

You see, dreams that seem impossible become invisible. When I ask people what they'd love to do and the answer is, "I don't have a clue," I know they're wrong. They think they're telling the truth, but they aren't. Everyone knows what they love. Most of us love many things. It just seems so totally impossible to do them (without starving to death) that dreams fall off the radar entirely and when we look at the screen, it's empty.

The purpose of presenting you with all these ideas—some a little wacky, some so good I bet you'll be doing them before long—is to make you realize that *you don't know what's possible!* Unless you know what's being done out in the real world, and what *could* be done, you'll never remember what you really want to do with this one wonderful life of yours.

And now you've heard of craftspeople using their homes for showrooms, of actors earning money in hospitals, and booklovers making good money on the lecture circuit, of people who want garden centers, spas, bed and breakfasts, animal refuges achieving their dreams without money! It's my dream that seeing those stories and those ideas has made a believer out of you: Yes, you can do what you love! Yes, you can do it without starving to death!

Be sure to read the Appendices that follow. If you've been circling words and assigning H-Levels to them, you're ready to run them through a simple but fantastic process I've created (and of which I am very proud) called Idea Soup, that will take you from these ideas to doing what you love, in just a few clear and easy steps. It works! So don't stop here, keep reading.

I hope you've enjoyed reading this book half as much as I've enjoyed writing it. I had too many ideas to put in one book so I've already started the second one. Keep your eye on my website (that's *www.barbarasher.com*) and on Genius Press too. Let's keep your mind open, active, having fun and open to all the amazing, creative, delightful possibilities that exist so you can do what you love.

APPENDIX 1

H-LEVELS

"Pleasure is a sign of the true functioning of our powers."
Marcel Proust

Many of us, when we go searching for our dreams and ways to support them, don't put happiness is high on the list. Or we assume that it must wait until other things have been taken care of. But the most successful people know that happiness is something you have to put into your life right this minute, the way you have to put gas in a car to make it go.

This deceptively simple method will guide you unerringly in the direction of what you really want and will help you avoid being sidetracked by what you 'should' want.

Any time you consider doing some activity or come across a new idea, ask yourself this KEY H-LEVEL QUESTION:

ON A SCALE OF ONE TO TEN, HOW HAPPY DOES THAT MAKE ME?

That's all you need to know to understand H-Levels. When you read anything in this book, keep a pencil nearby and circle anything that seems to have an H-Level of 7 or above. When you're finished you can go back and look at what you've noted and it will tell you a lot about what you want, and what your gifts are.

Making a practice of the pursuit of happiness is a craft. You need to know that happiness is what you want and that it's not only allowed, it's essential. Using happiness to determine what you should be doing with your life is the smartest and most practical thing you can do. Why? Because what you love is what you are gifted at. Any activity that makes you happy is using your talents. Your only job is to find out what makes you happy. Being constantly aware of H-Levels will soon show you exactly what that is.

APPENDIX 2
IDEA SOUP

You'll be happy to know I have devised a very powerful (and easy) system for figuring out exactly what you want to do. Just put anything you enjoy through these steps:

1) Name anything you enjoy (or ever did). That means it had an H-Level of 7 or above.

2) Ask yourself: what do/did you love most about that activity? (Again, what you pick must have at least an H-Level of 7 or above.)

3) What would you most like to avoid in this activity, or in your life in general?

4) What resources are available to you? (Do you have a van? A spare room? Speak Swahili? Have plenty of time or enough money to get by for a while?)

5) Take your answers to an Idea Party (instructions are in Appendix 3—Idea Parties). Remember, this book is one kind of idea party, so be sure to look through to see if I've included something that requires a van, Swahili, etc.

6) Create a support team for yourself to keep you moving, step by step, until you reach your goal. (Instructions are in Appendix 4—Support Systems.)

APPENDIX 3

IDEA PARTIES

They sound great, don't they, even if you're not sure what an Idea Party is? Here's how you do it...

1. FIND GOOD PEOPLE

Each time that you meet someone you'd like to know better, give that person your name and phone number and invite them to your Idea Party, even if you don't yet have a date or location. Hopefully, you'll collect a few new names and phone numbers. Call everyone. The first person you speak with can be your buddy. She'll help you pick the date and location and call people she knows. Don't hesitate to ask your friends, family and coworkers to come to your Idea Party. Just say, "I'm having an Idea Party. Want to come?" and you'll get surprisingly positive results. You can have as many as 15 or 20 people at this party, and the more varied their backgrounds, the better. NEVER PERSUADE ANYONE TO COME. You only want people who want to be there. That usually screens out the "show-me" types, who don't make the best brainstormers.

2. TELL EVERYONE TO BRING FOOD AND SEND THEM STRAIGHT TO THE KITCHEN

I strongly advise that the party be potluck. When people arrive, they'll break the ice best by going straight to the kitchen and putting out their food on the dishes you've provided. This will give everyone the feeling of working together right from the beginning. Also, bustling around in the kitchen looking for the right utensils creates an atmosphere that is a perfect warm-up for an Idea Party: playful, informal, with easy problems to solve.

3. BEGIN THE BRAINSTORMING

After everyone has a plate and is sitting (on couches and chairs, the floor, or around a big table), the brainstorming begins. Have pads of paper and pencils available. One by one, each person can ask for some help with brainstorming (or feel free to pass if they choose). Here's what they will say:

"Here is my wish:_____,

and here is my obstacle:_____."

Each speaker should present only one wish and one major obstacle. Explain as little as possible, so there's plenty of time to get suggestions. Each person gets 5 minutes unless there are fewer than 6 people, then they get 10 minutes. You want to keep the pace snappy.

4. TIMEKEEPER'S TIPS

Don't worry if there doesn't seem to be enough time; everyone can talk after the brainstorming when they break for dessert and coffee. Timekeeper's tip: use a timer, one that makes a loud "Ding!" when the time is up. You don't want to be the bad guy who stops people from talking. BUT IF EVERYBODY TAKES TOO MUCH TIME, SOMEONE WON'T GET THEIR CHANCE. The whole brainstorming shouldn't last more than 1½ hours. If you'd like more instructions on how to brainstorm, see page 126 in *Wishcraft*, my first book.

5. BREAK FOR DESSERT

After everyone has had a chance to get ideas, the brainstorming is over. But the party goes on. Return to the food table for dessert or coffee. This is when people will get to know each other. By this time, they'll have some questions for each other, or more advice than they had time for during the brainstorming. Be sure to leave enough time for this part of the evening. It's an important part of the process.

6. FINALE

When the evening is over, expect to get compliments on this party, because Idea Parties are fun! Ask people to leave their names and numbers if they want to be called for the next Idea Party. And if they want to host an Idea Party themselves, that's great! Go to their house next time!

7. THROW ANOTHER IDEA PARTY IN A MONTH-AND WATCH YOUR LIFE GET BETTER.

At every Idea Party, you'll meet new people. Idea Parties are a sensational way to get to know the best people in town, and a warm and stimulating way to do some first class networking. Never underestimate the difference it can make in your life to meet someone who can hand you a piece to your puzzle. You could find out something that changes your life in this best and oldest way of socializing.

8. FORGET SELF-IMPROVEMENT

Isolation is the dream killer. You don't need a positive attitude or self-confidence to make your dreams come true. You just need a lot of friends who want to see you get your dreams. With that support, your world will turn around.

I often have idea parties on the telephone. Get on my mailing list so you'll know when they're scheduled. Go to www.barbarasher.com and click on "mailing list" and sign up. Your name will never be given to anyone else. Promise!

APPENDIX 4

SUPPORT TEAMS

What follows is a streamlined version of the Buddy System, my technique of joining forces with one or more friends to meet your goals. Whereas a Success Team typically has six members and meets once a week for two hours, the Buddy System allows you to use the same principles on a smaller scale.

1. PICK A BUDDY

The person you pick can be your best friend, but she or he can also be someone you know casually from work or aerobics class. Some people are happiest working with a bosom friend; others find a close personal relationship too competitive or too cozy for business. Your buddy SHOULD be someone you respect and can count on to stick to a short-term commitment. She or he can be working in the same field as you (as two actresses I know who rehearse and brace each other for auditions), but it's at least as much fun if your goals are wildly different.

2. WEEKLY BUSINESS MEETING

Agree to meet with your "buddy" each week for at least one hour at a regular time. At first, this may seem like just one more demand on your poor schedule, but you'll find that the hour will immediately pay for itself in increased energy and efficiency. Each of you should keep one rule firmly in mind. For one hour, you're not going to talk about the great movie you saw last week, or the coming elections; you're going to stick to business. The temptation to socialize will be great. Use a timer, and resist it.

3. PICK A GOAL

At your first meeting, each of you should set a first goal that seems reachable within three to eighteen months (depending on how long you're willing to commit yourself to work together), such as "get a raise," "make up a portfolio and slides and show art galleries," or "sell at least one of my needlepoint designs to a boutique." Pick a goal you really want, even if it seems improbable or scary—not something you feel lukewarm and safe about. Your desire to achieve the goal will be your chief energy source. On the other hand, don't aim too high too soon. If you've never drawn a line in your life, "become a commercial artist" is too big a goal to shoot for; "enter and successfully complete a life drawing class" would be more like it.

4. SET TARGET DATES ON A POCKET CALENDAR

You can always change the dates if they turn out to be unrealistic, but you have to have them or you'll procrastinate. The later of your two target dates is your joint target date. You'll agree to keep meeting until both your goals are met.

5. PLAN BACKWARD TO THE FIRST STEPS

Starting at your goal, plan backward ("Before I can go to medical school, I have to apply and get in; before I can do that I have to pass pre-med courses; before I can do that I have to find and enroll in a college that gives them at night"), until you arrive at something small and manageable that you can do within the coming week to set you on the path to your goal ("This week I will request catalogs from all the local colleges").

If you have a creative goal, such as writing a children's story, make your "first steps" small enough so that you'll do them. The point is to get

248

moving. Carol, the head of personnel in a major department store, was confident in her job, but timid when it came to her lifelong dream of learning to paint. She doubted that she had enough talent and was reluctant even to try. Her buddy, Donna, a secretary and would-be city planner, cheerfully gave her her first week's assignment. "Bring in five bad drawings of your cat. And they'd better be bad!" The assignment got Carol laughing—and drawing. Enrolling in a class would come later.

6. SCHEDULE FIRST STEPS FOR SPECIFIC DAYS AND TIMES IN THE COMING WEEK

If either of you has something especially difficult to do, which you might be tempted to avoid, schedule a morale-booster call from your buddy for right beforehand. (You can call him or her back afterward and say, "I did it!") Booster calls should be limited to three minutes, out of respect for the value of each of your time frames. (In real emergencies, though, your buddy might be willing to come with you right to the interviewers door, or sit in the next room working on his or her goal while you practice the cello.)

7. THINK THROUGH OR REHEARSE ANY UNFAMILIAR THINGS YOU'LL HAVE TO DO

How long will it take you to dress, and get to the audition? What are you going to say in that phone call or job interview? We often think we lack some mysterious thing called "self-confidence," when the real problem is that we don't know what we're doing. Advise each other on how to be informed and prepared. You'll find that you have more common sense for each other than you do for yourself.

Now you are both ready to go into action—promise to report the results to each other at the next meeting. You've just done something very important. You've created a structure of expectation outside yourself that will help keep you on track. As it's much easier to do something when you've got a boss, a teacher, a deadline, your buddy is set up to expect you to do the things you want to do, but wouldn't do just for yourself.

8. SECOND BUSINESS MEETING (AND ALL SUBSEQUENT MEETINGS): REMEMBER, NO SOCIALIZING UNTIL BUSINESS IS OVER

Using a clock or timer, each of you gets half an hour. For the first five minutes, report on what you did (or didn't do) and what the results were; then talk about any problems you ran into, or ways you're stymied about what to do next. You may need to divide this problem-solving time into two parts:

Creative Planning: If you're discouraged, depressed, or scared, you may not be able to solve practical problems until you get negative feelings out of the way. so if you need to, take ten minutes or less to gripe your heart out. Make it as mean, low-down, dirty, and even funny as you can. "I hate my goal. I'm going to give it all up and run away with the exterminator." During this time, your buddy should simply listen, or cheer you on—not try to cheer you up. When you feel better, you can move on...

Brainstorming: You and your buddy should now come up with as many inventive solutions to your problem(s) as you can, including outrageous ones. Don't censor. You can always weed out the "joke" ideas late—even they often contain the seeds of brilliant solutions. Legitimate subjects for brainstorming include: how to raise money; how to get inexpensive, or free, equipment, materials, or services; how to solve the problem of child care; and anything else you can think of.

Sara, a painter on a tight budget, who wished she could buy a house with lots of studio space, brainstormed with two friends, and they came up with these ideas:

- Join forces with other artists to rent a big house.
- Find a dilapidated house the city is selling cheap, and fix it up.
- Enter all the sweepstakes that have a house as a prize (joke idea—but some competitions do award property to whoever writes the best essay sent in with a small entry fee).
- Find a lonely, old person in a large house who needs a companion.
- Offer to be a caretaker on someone's country property.

As it turned out, one of Sara's friends knew someone who had a house in the country. Sara's friend called the man, who said he already had a caretaker—but he had a neighbor in the country who traveled a lot, and who might let Sara live and paint in his house if she would take care of his dogs.

9. SCHEDULE

Save the last five minutes of your half-hour to plan out and write in your calendar what you'll be doing the next week.

10. EXPANDING THE GROUP

Once the "Buddy System" starts working, there's no reason you have to confine it to just the two of you. If two heads are better than one, how about more? (If you have more people, of course, you must limit their time to fifteen minutes or so.)

About Barbara Sher

Barbara Sher is a business owner, career counselor, and the bestselling author of five books on goal achievement and teamwork. She has presented her seminars and workshops on teambuilding, goal-achievement and negotiation skills to people across North America and Europe.

She has appeared on national and local radio and television, including Oprah, The Donahue Show, The Today Show, 60 Minutes, CNN and Good Morning America.

Her first book *Wishcraft: How to Get What You Really Want* has sold well over a million copies. In 1972, Sher invented Success Teams—small groups in which members work together in weekly meetings to identify their dreams and help each other make them come true. The teams were an instant hit. By 1976, she was running workshops to help people create Success Teams throughout the United States and Europe. Today, Sher's teams are operating in universities, career centers, Fortune 500 companies and in entrepreneur associations in Nepal, Siberia, Israel, Canada, Thailand, Australia, and Bulgaria.

When Sher discovered that many people didn't know what they'd really love to do, she began hosting problem-solving sessions, developing dozens of powerful techniques that freed people from "goal-paralysis." These techniques have been developed in all her following books, workshops, tapes and courses.

Her third book, The New York Times best-seller, *I Could Do Anything if I Only Knew What It Was*, an explosive bestseller was followed in 1996 by *Live the Life You Love in Ten Easy Step-by-Step Lessons*, which won the first award ever given for "Best Motivational Book of the Year" by the Books For A Better Life Award Commission.

Her fifth book, *It's Only Too Late If You Don't Start Now, How to Create Your Second Life at Any Age,* has turned ideas of midlife on their ear and her hilarious hour-long PBS special by the same name has been submitted for an Emmy nomination and is winning accolades wherever it is shown.

Two more PBS specials have followed: "Live the Life You Love/Map to Success," a two-part show and "Barbara Sher's Idea Party." All three of her shows have been called "standup comedy with a message."

Presently, Barbara Sher consults with clients in her New York office, speaks in front of organizations around the world and travels to her second home in Central Turkey where she has started a foundation called Hands on Hips, Inc., to teach e-commerce to the village weavers.

You can find more information at www.barbarasher.com

WRITE ME!

Have you got a great idea you'd like to share with world? Or a story about yourself or someone you know who went after their dreams in an unusual or original way? Open your inventive mind and tell me your ideas and stories. Let the world know your ideas, what you've done, what someone else has done, or what you think somebody really *ought* to do.

I'll read your letter personally and if I can use it in my next book, I'll contact you at once to get your release (or you can include permission right in your letter). What will you get in return? If I use your idea I'll send you a free copy of the next book, I'll put your name in it, right after your entry (unless you want to stay anonymous) and you will have the satisfaction of knowing that you have probably helped someone make their "impossible" dream come true.

I'd love to hear from you. You can write me at

Barbara Sher
Box 20052
Park West Station
New York, New York 10025

or email me at : sher@geniuspress.com

Thank you,
Barbara Sher

TO ORDER BARBARA'S BOOKS AND TAPES

I'm adding new titles every month. To find everything and stay up to date, come to www.barbarasher.com or www.geniuspress.com.

Here's what's available now:

Books

Wishcraft

I Could Do Anything if I Only Knew What It Was

Live the Life You Love

It's Only Too Late If You Don't Start Now

(All these titles can be found on amazon.com or at your local bookstore.)

Courses

Dare to Live Your Dream, a 12-audiocassette course

Discover Your Dream Course Workbook with audio CD

Making Dreams Happen, a 23-CD set with Barbara Sher, Barbara Winter and Valerie Young

(Come to www.barbarasher.com or www.geniuspress.com for these audio courses.)

Videos

Barbara's PBS shows can presently be yours by pledging your support to your local public television station. Check to see if they're airing Barbara's show in your town (and if they plan to bring her out to do a workshop!) These videos will become available to the public on Barbara's websites when they are no longer being used as pledge gifts.

For more information: order@geniuspress.com